KU-438-718

For Sammy, Kush, Yash and my family.
Thank you for always inspiring me.

Dr Chintal's
KITCHEN

Quick, easy, healthy meals the whole family will love

Dr Chintal Patel

First published in 2024 by
Palazzo Editions Ltd
Marine House, Tide Mill Way,
Woodbridge, Suffolk IP12 1AP

www.palazzoeditions.com

Text © 2024 Dr Chintal Patel

Please note that the information provided here is for general informational purposes only and is not intended as personalised medical or nutrition advice. It should not be used to diagnose or treat any medical or nutrition condition or to replace advice from your healthcare provider. The content is accurate and up to date at the time of writing, but medical and nutritional knowledge is constantly evolving and new research may supersede or alter the information presented here. Always consult with a qualified healthcare professional about any medical concerns or questions you may have.

Hardback ISBN 9781786751461
eBook ISBN 9781786751645

All rights reserved. No part of this publication may be reproduced in any form or by any means – electronic, mechanical, photocopying, recording or otherwise – or stored in any retrieval system of any nature without prior written permission from the copyright-holders.

Dr Chintal Patel has asserted her moral right to be identified as the author of this work in accordance with the Copyright, Designs and Patents Act of 1988.

A CIP catalogue record for this book is available from the British Library.

Every reasonable effort has been made to trace copyright-holders of material reproduced in this book, but if any have been inadvertently overlooked the publishers would be glad to hear from them.

Designed by Andrew Barron @thextension

Edited by Helena Caldon

All original photography by Dr Chintal Patel

Printed in China

10 9 8 7 6 5 4 3 2 1

Foreword

I am a huge advocate of healthy eating and encouraging our children to grow up eating a wholesome diet, whilst enjoying the process at the same time.

I have known Chintal and followed her recipe blog for the past five years. I love the way she combines her professional knowledge as a doctor with creating nutritious family food that is not only appealing to the eye but also tastes delicious.

Dr Chintal's book encourages families to open up conversations around food and get cooking in the kitchen together. It allows children the freedom to experiment with ideas and recipes, encouraging a healthy relationship with food from an early age.

Dr Chintal has the insight and direct experience of the importance of family health and its link to food through her work as a doctor within the NHS, as well as through being a working mum.

Her book addresses the urgent problem of obesity in children and the importance of eating healthily together in a fun and engaging way that is also time efficient.

There can be no better antidote to the rush, screens and pressures of modern life than quality time as a family around the table. Dr Chintal helps that time be as enjoyable, healthy and easy as possible.

I am delighted to support Dr Chintal and her fantastic book!

Dr Rangan Chatterjee

Contents

Introduction

Welcome to a culinary journey through the heart of my home, where you will find a treasure trove of everyday recipes with a single aim: to make cooking and eating at home as easy and nutritious as possible.

I've specifically developed these recipes with the demands of modern life in mind. Whether you're a busy professional, a parent juggling a hundred demands, or simply someone looking to make quick, simple, nutritious meals, this book will become your trusted kitchen companion.

I've taken the guesswork out of meal planning. If you're short of time, turn to the 15-minute Meals chapter. Need a nourishing dinner without any fuss? Explore the world of Time-saving Traybakes. Or when you're ready for a culinary adventure, dive into Friday-night Feasts. There is a recipe for every occasion and something to tempt every palate.

You'll find a vegetarian option for every dish and I've maximised nutrition without compromising on flavour. I'll start with the theory of nutrition. The focus is always on eating well without restrictions, without calorie counting, without adhering to any fad diet – just good, wholesome, balanced meals. My overarching message is that instead of restricting or removing food groups from your diet, you should focus more on what you can include, what you can *add* to your plate. Then, everything else – from optimum nutrition to health and well-being – will fall into place.

Putting nutritional theory into practice doesn't have to be complicated. Even a simple, 15-minute meal made from store-cupboard ingredients can still be delicious, nutritious and balanced. This is more than just a cookbook: it is a guide to family-friendly cooking and nutrition, written by a doctor, who understands the real-life challenges of working parents who have to feed (sometimes) fussy young eaters.

I would love this to become the recipe book you turn to daily for inspiration and guidance, flecked with turmeric and all the colours of the rainbow, with every other page earmarked as a family favourite. Join me on a journey where good food meets good health and every meal is a celebration of both.

A bit about me

I'm an African-born, English- and Gujarati-speaking British Indian (that's a mouthful!). I am a wife to Sameet and a mum to two beautiful boys aged thirteen and eleven. I have worked as an NHS doctor in the heart of central London for over twenty years.

As a child, I was always 'cooking'. From helping my mum in the kitchen to making mud pies and rose-petal perfume in the garden, preparing dishes has always been an integral part of my life. I have so many happy memories of special moments that centre around food! My earliest childhood memory is of our family kitchen when I was growing up in Tanzania. We had a walk-in pantry with shelves from floor to ceiling filled with provisions. In the corner was a stool, and on the shelf just above that strategically placed stool was where the jaggery was stored. If you haven't heard of jaggery, it is an unrefined sugar used in Indian cooking. I would creep in when no one was looking, spoon in hand, to enjoy a sneaky sweet treat! If you haven't tried it,

OPPOSITE My beloved kitchen set: the only childhood toy which came with me to England.

Growing up, our mealtimes were always protected family time. After our move to London, times were hard. My parents both worked more than full-time in order to provide for us, as they had had to leave almost everything behind in East Africa. The evening meal was the only time we could all be together. Most days my dad would come home from work to eat with us and then return to work. This was our storytelling time when we shared daily episodes of our lives and connected over a home-cooked meal. My mum always made food from scratch. I still marvel at how efficient and organised she must have been. Family storytelling always started as we prepared the food. At the time, if I'm honest, I did it because I had to; all of us chipping in was a means of getting dinner on the table quickly. However, looking back, this little girl was learning how recipes came together through patience and skill to create delicious meals. At the same time, she was accumulating the wisdom and techniques handed down through generations, which truly made the cooking experience unique. She was learning about the importance of meal prepping, of the fusion of spices, the technique of rolling the perfect *rotli*, and it's because of this I am able to teach these same skills to my own children and in my cooking classes. I would love to keep alive these traditions of cooking together as a family through my cookbooks.

please do – it is absolutely delicious! I can still picture exactly where it was stored in our pantry.

Sadly, we have very few photographs from this time, as my parents had to leave behind almost all our belongings when their business was seized due to nationalisation and we were forced to leave Tanzania. I was allowed to bring just one toy – my beloved Indian kitchen set, housed in a rather odd-looking doll with a secret zip compartment. I have only a fragment left of the original set, as it has been well-loved and played with not only by me, but also my own children.

On Saturdays, my sister and I helped in our family business. Even this centred around food! My parents owned a grocery store in a small village in Hampshire, where we were the only Indian family. My parents were very proud of their culture and raised

us to celebrate it. They even introduced an Indian section in their store, full of spices and Asian ingredients. Remember, this was many years ago, before the large supermarkets were selling any speciality Indian foods. My dad was well ahead of his time in introducing an entire range of Indian ingredients and spices that reached from floor to ceiling, from *papads* and pickles to *dhokra* mixes – our family shop had it all!

Every Sunday, when the shop was closed, we made the weekly trip to Wembley and Southall in London. This was the nearest place to buy Indian groceries, so my dad was quite right that there was a gap in the market. I feel like he initially stocked everything in his shop just so he could continue to eat his favourite foods throughout the week!

To begin with, the Indian section in our shop wasn't that well received; it was seen as an odd thing to have, given that we were the only Indian family in the village. However, as my parents shared their culinary wisdom, tips and recipe ideas, word spread far and wide. Shoppers travelled from miles away to visit our small corner shop (yes, it actually was on a corner – in an L-shape, to be exact) to buy Indian ingredients. I am so proud of how my parents celebrated their heritage in the face of adversity and took a risk in stocking Indian ingredients. Over time, these ingredients connected the local community to our culinary heritage as they engaged with the stories and recipes shared by my family. I am excited to keep that tradition alive. Whilst this isn't an Indian recipe book, my Indian heritage and love of spices will hopefully shine through.

Another thing I remember vividly growing up is that I always saw my parents playing an equal role in the kitchen, which isn't always the case in South-Asian culture. My papa cooked together with my mum and he also made the best packed lunches, because his sandwiches were incredibly adventurous, always with an Indian twist. My friends certainly felt envious of them! My parents also encouraged us to take an active role in the kitchen, where we worked as a team. One of us would initiate the prep, the second cooked, the third cleared up and the fourth . . . tasted. My sister would always try to ensure that she was the taster! Our roles overlapped and changed, but, essentially, it was the four of us in the kitchen, all working together as a team. As a mother of two sons,

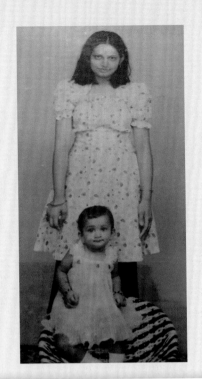

My parents and me in Tanzania in about 1978.

I have continued to instil equality in the kitchen, and I hope my sons will continue this with their own families.

Food has played a significant part in every stage of my life. Even after I had left home, I remember my mum feeding most of the students in my university halls during my first year at medical school. At the weekends, my parents would deliver huge containers of curries to last me the week. However, this delivery was quickly devoured by my friends. I know they looked forward to my parents visiting just as much as I did! Sharing food is the Indian way; we show love through food. I love how people can bond through recipes and how they continue to enjoy the same recipes for years to come. One of my university flatmates was introduced to Indian food for the very first time through my mum's curry deliveries. She absolutely loved them and slowly started experimenting with ingredients and cooking her own Indian meals. That same friend now cooks the best Indian curries for her own children! Food is connection, in every way.

As an NHS GP in central London, I work with many families from all socio-economic backgrounds and in every ethnic group. I understand the need for family-friendly food that is accessible, affordable, easy to make and enjoyed by the whole family. I often meet parents who struggle to encourage their children to eat nutritious meals, usually due to a lack of time, basic nutritional knowledge and cooking skills. They find themselves either cooking separate meals for their children or buying ready-made meals. Through the recipes in my book, social-media videos and cookery classes, my aim has always been to empower families to cook together, to enjoy nutritious food and to save time and money. As a doctor and a mum, I know just how important good nutrition is for children in every way and at every stage of their lives.

As a working mother of two boys, I can empathise with my patients trying to feed a family with differing palates and with limited time. Both my boys have been fussy eaters at times and we still have days when things aren't plain sailing. I always encourage them to join in in the kitchen as my sous-chefs. Now, aged thirteen and eleven, they are in charge of weekend breakfast in our house so my husband and I are treated to a lie-in once a week!

There are so many benefits to cooking with children. I encourage you to embrace the mess and to cook meals together whenever you can. These recipes have been designed to allow children to safely get involved and have fun in the kitchen, encouraging them to form a healthy relationship with food from a young age. Cooking from an early age is also the perfect way to help children develop their sensory and motor skills. It can be educational – teaching problem-solving, maths and organisational skills – and is a wonderful way of encouraging children to be creative in the kitchen. It's also an important life skill for children, setting them up for living independently, at university and beyond.

I'll share time-saving kitchen hacks and tips in my book. I love creating recipes using new ingredients to expand my children's tastes, and I am keen to encourage other families to do the same.

Nutrition: The Basics

Nutritional advice can be confusing, with a multitude of conflicting ideas and diets circulating on social media, some endorsed by celebrities with huge platforms. How do you navigate this vast ocean of information, trying to determine what is misinformation and to make the right choices for yourself and your family? This has always been an area of personal interest for me, something I've committed to studying for my own benefit as well as in my medical practice.

Once I became a mother, I was acutely aware of how crucial nutrition is for child health. This awareness was fuelled by alarming child-health statistics, including dental issues,[1] childhood obesity rates,[2] and a surge in cases of childhood type-2 diabetes.[3] I grew increasingly determined to provide my children, and those of my patients, with the best possible start in life, to help them build a healthy relationship with food.

Surprisingly, when I was at medical school very little attention was paid to nutrition. My training covered only the basics. It's quite shocking, really, how little time was dedicated to lifestyle education, especially considering how lifestyle factors, particularly diet, can profoundly affect our health in so many ways. It's been heartening to witness the recent publication of a nutrition curriculum for UK medical students[4], as well as education programmes like culinary medicine emerging as effective ways to increase health professionals' confidence in addressing nutrition, to help prevent and treat patients' medical conditions.[5]

My aim is to share nutritional facts and theories based on real, scientifically-proven evidence derived from large studies that follow hundreds of thousands of people to give a more accurate picture. I aim to provide insights not only as a doctor, but also as a patient and a parent. These are common questions that regularly come up in my clinic that I've asked myself, too. But bear in mind that this chapter is just a starting point. There are many factors that affect the types of meals families enjoy and it's impossible to cover everything in just a few pages. What this chapter can do, though, is provide evidence-based *facts* to help you make your own informed choices and provide some options for how you can easily put nutritional theory into practice.

My aim is to alleviate any concerns regarding nutrition, so we can shift our focus in the rest of the book to the fun part: creating easy, delicious and nutritious meals. My recipes don't exclude any food groups – personally, I enjoy all foods in moderation – my approach emphasises adding variety to *enhance* your diet, instead of restricting certain foods.

What are macro- and micronutrients?

Let's begin with the fundamentals. Macronutrients are the substances that your body requires in substantial (macro) quantities to provide us with energy, to support growth and development, health and well-being. Micronutrients are equally essential for optimal bodily functioning but are required in smaller (micro) amounts. These include vitamins and minerals and are found within the macronutrients in your diet.

OPPOSITE Hosting a family nutrition workshop with Kush and Yash.

The three main macronutrients are carbohydrates, fats and proteins. It's vital to note that none of these should be entirely removed from a healthy balanced diet; all three are essential for overall health. The key lies in finding the right balance of these within a varied, high-quality diet. This can help you to feel full after a meal; to manage hunger; to maintain energy levels; to maintain muscles; balance blood sugars; and support physical and mental well-being.

Carbohydrates

Carbohydrates are found in a variety of foods and exist in numerous forms. They serve as a crucial fuel source for our bodies as they are converted into glucose. Although it is technically possible to convert glucose from fats and proteins, carbohydrates are the human body's preferred source of energy. Foods containing carbohydrates are also valuable sources of fibre and other micronutrients, particularly B vitamins.

Many people express concerns about consuming too many carbohydrates, commonly referred to as 'carbs'. Lower-carbohydrate diets can be beneficial for certain medical conditions such as type-2 diabetes,[6] however, for the majority of people, carbohydrates can be an integral part of a healthy and balanced diet. The emphasis should be on quality. After all, as one famous American nutritionist once said, carbohydrates can be anything from lollipops to lentils.[7]

Carbohydrates can be categorised into two main groups: whole carbohydrates and refined carbohydrates. Whole carbohydrates are minimally processed and retain the natural dietary fibre found in food sources. They include whole grains, vegetables, beans and legumes, such as lentils. Whenever possible, opt for whole-grain carbohydrates or, if eating starchy foods like potatoes, leave the skin on to increase your fibre intake.

Whole grains are the seeds of cereal plants such as wheat, barley and rye. They have had very little removed in processing and contain all three parts of the grain, so they contain a wide range of nutrients. Diets rich in whole grains have been linked to a lower risk of heart disease, type-2 diabetes, some types of cancer and obesity.[8,9] Examples of whole grains include oats, whole wheat, brown rice, rye and quinoa; they are also found in foods made with these ingredients, such as whole-grain bread and pasta.

Eating whole grains is also a great way of getting more fibre into your diet. Simple tips to increase whole grains in your diet include:

○ Swap refined foods for whole-grain foods such as brown bread or pasta instead of white, or try a mix of both to begin with.
○ Oats or oat flour make a delicious alternative to white flour in baking (see my Blueberry & Cinnamon Banana Bread recipe on p. 169).
○ If you enjoy cereal for breakfast, switch to whole-grain varieties (but watch out for sugar and salt content), or try porridge made with oats and/or quinoa.
○ Try adding whole grains such as bulgur or quinoa to soups and salads.
○ Mix it up! Try bulgur, couscous or quinoa instead of rice with your curry or stew.

Glycaemic index

Starchy vegetables such as potatoes, sweet potatoes, yams and plantains are also sources of carbohydrates. Sweet potato, yam and plantain are broken down into sugar more slowly compared with white potatoes. The speed at which carbohydrate foods are broken down to sugar is known as the glycaemic index (GI). Sugary carbohydrates have a high glycaemic index, while more complex carbohydrates, such as lentils and sweet potatoes, have a low glycaemic index. Cooking methods also make a difference. For example, mashed potato has a higher GI than unpeeled, boiled new potatoes. Don't forget to count starchy vegetables as carbohydrates rather than vegetables in your 'five a day' and try to enjoy these starchy vegetables with their skins on to lower the GI and to retain more of their fibre, vitamins and minerals. Low-GI diets have been linked to improved blood-sugar levels and can be beneficial in the treatment of polycystic ovarian syndrome (PCOS)[10] and type-1 and type-2 diabetes.[11]

Refined carbohydrates are carbohydrates that have been processed, resulting in the loss of fibre, vitamins and minerals. They often have additional sugar, salt or other additives to preserve flavour. Examples of refined carbohydrates include white bread or pastries, sweetened drinks, white rice and many breakfast cereals. These foods are examples of ultra-processed foods, which we will cover in depth later.

Refined carbs have a higher GI, which means they increase insulin and blood sugar levels more quickly, resulting in subsequent crashes in blood sugar. Refined high-GI foods have been linked to increased hunger and may lead to food cravings.[12] You don't have to remove refined carbohydrates completely from your diet, but try to get most of your carbohydrates from whole foods. Don't feel you have to drastically change everything in your diet; just make a small, sustainable change each week or over a period of time that works for you. This is often much more effective and easier to maintain in the long term than taking the drastic step of cutting out refined foods altogether. My aim is not to scare you into thinking that all refined carbs are bad. They're not, and I regularly use them in my recipes. It's all about balance. Enjoy everything in moderation, switch it up to healthier options when you can and work on what you can *add* to your diet rather than what you remove.

Sugars

Sugars are a type of carbohydrate found in many forms in our diet, sometimes naturally in our food – in milk, fruits and vegetables, for example. They can also be found as 'free sugars', examples of which are granulated or 'table' sugar and honey. Sugars are also found in fruit juices, biscuits, chocolate, fizzy drinks and so on.

There has been growing concern for many decades about the amount of free sugar consumed by adults and children. Eating too much sugar can cause tooth decay and weight gain.[1,2]

Too much high-GI sugary food in the diet can affect our physical and mental health. Sugar is easily absorbed and digested, leading to increased insulin levels and potential swings in blood-glucose levels, which can affect energy levels, leaving you feeling fatigued and hungry. They can also lead to overeating and weight gain.

Current Public Health England guidelines are that free sugars should not make up more than 5% of the energy (calories) you get from food and drink each day.[13] As a rough guide this means:

○ Age 4 or less – avoid all drinks and food sweetened with added sugar.
○ Age 4–6 – no more than 19g a day (5 tsp).
○ Age 7–10 – no more than 24g a day (6 tsp).
○ Adults – no more than 30g a day (7 tsp).

In reality, in the UK most adults and children are consuming way above this recommended amount. If you know that one can of cola can contain up to 9 teaspoons of sugar, or one chocolate bar around 6 teaspoons of sugar, you can see how easy it is to tip over this suggested daily allowance.

There is also a lot of confusion around recipes and how sugar is portrayed online. A particular bugbear for me is when I see recipes promoted as 'healthy' because they have 'no refined sugar'. However, those same recipes will often use copious quantities of maple or other syrup, honey or fruit juice to sweeten the dish. This is all still free sugar.

You might look at the label on a pot of plain yoghurt and see as much as 8g of sugar per serving. But none of these are free sugars; they all come from milk. The same principle applies to an individual portion of fruit. For instance, an apple may contain about 11g of total sugar, depending on size,

variety and ripeness. However, the sugar in whole fruits is not classified as free sugar unless the fruit is juiced or puréed. Fruit generally has a low GI, which means the sugar takes longer to digest into blood sugar. A plain yoghurt and an apple would still be a healthier choice than a food containing lots of free sugars, even if the two products contained the same amount of total sugar.

The sugars found naturally in fruit and vegetables are less likely to cause tooth decay because they are contained within the structure of the fruit or vegetable, but when they are blended or juiced, the sugars are released and can damage teeth.

Free sugars do make food taste delicious and a lot of people, myself included, enjoy free sugars as part of a healthy, balanced diet. However, we should be focusing on getting most of our calories from other types of foods, such as whole grains, starchy foods and fruits and vegetables, while enjoying sugary foods occasionally and in moderation.

Practical ways you can reduce sugar in your diet include:

○ Cook your meals from scratch as often as you can. Ready-made meals and takeaways often contain a lot of sugar and salt.
○ Check labels – the traffic-light system of labelling in the UK makes it very easy to spot high-sugar 'red' labels, but check the back of the packet too, and look at 'carbohydrates of which sugars'. This tells you more about the free sugars in a food. Ideally, aim for products that contain less than 5g of sugar per 100g.

○ Reduce (to less than 150ml a day) or cut out fruit juices and smoothies from your diet. Have them with a meal to reduce the risk of tooth decay.

○ Swap out fizzy or sugary drinks with water or milk.

○ Swap sugary cereals for whole-grain cereals or enjoy homemade porridge for breakfast.

○ Stop adding sugar to tea and coffee.

○ Swap fruit yoghurts for natural yoghurts.

○ If buying tinned fruit, buy fruit in its own juice rather than in syrup.

○ Swap sugary snacks, such as biscuits and cakes, for crackers, oatcakes, rice cakes and nuts.

○ Ask yourself, do you *really* need to have dessert every day?

Why is fibre important?

Dietary fibre, which is found exclusively in plant-based foods, plays a crucial role in maintaining good health and well-being. Fibre is the indigestible part of these foods that passes through our digestive system largely intact. Whilst it might not provide calories or essential nutrients, it has a huge impact on our health by helping to maintain bowel health, partly through supporting a healthy gut microbiome. Fibre contributes to regular bowel movements; helps to control blood-sugar levels;[14] may play a role in reducing cholesterol;[15] and plays a vital role in maintaining a healthy weight.[16] Eating fibre is associated with a decreased risk of bowel cancer;[17] may be associated with a decreased risk of heart disease or stroke;[18] and a lower risk of developing type-2 diabetes.[19]

Public Health England guidelines suggest a daily dietary intake of fibre[13] of between 15g for 2–5-year-olds and 30g for over-16s.

In the UK, statistics show that we are not getting enough fibre in our diets.[20] So how can we do this? We should be eating as many plant-based foods as possible! Here are a few of my favourite ways to do this:

○ Try eating vegetables like potatoes, carrots and parsnips with the skin on.

○ Choose whole grains whenever possible, like brown rice, quinoa or bulgur as an alternative to white rice, or whole-wheat pasta over white pasta.

○ Add pulses and beans like lentils and chickpeas to curries, soups, stews and salads.

○ Add a side salad or a side dish of vegetables to every meal.

○ Upgrade your snacks – vegetable sticks, hummus, nuts, seeds and oatcakes are all high-fibre, healthy snacks.

○ Enjoy fruits, berries and dried fruits as puddings.

○ Enjoy oats or quinoa porridge for breakfast or, if you prefer cereals, choose a high-fibre cereal such as Shredded Wheat or Weetabix. Check labels on cereals as they can have a lot of added sugar and salt, as well as other additives.

Once again, focus on variety and what you can *add* to your diet, rather than what you restrict or remove.

Fat

Dietary fat is needed for energy as well as various bodily functions. It is essential for the absorption of fat-soluble vitamins A, D, E and K. Fats are also an important source of energy and are needed to build and repair cell walls and our brains.

However, problems can arise when we eat too much fat, or the wrong types of fats. We can broadly label fats as 'unsaturated' or 'saturated' fats.

Although foods can contain a mixture of unsaturated and saturated fat, meat and animal products such as dairy tend to be higher in saturated fats. Plant-based foods high in saturated fats include palm oil and coconut oil. Ultra-processed foods such as fatty meats; processed meats, such as sausages and pies; cheeses; ghee, butter and lard; cream; chocolate; and biscuits, cakes and pastries are particularly high in saturated fats. Generally, diets high in saturated fat are linked to increased LDL cholesterol in the blood. Often labelled as 'bad', LDL cholesterol has been associated with an increased risk of heart disease and stroke.[21] However, not all saturated fats are equal, with more recent evidence suggesting the type of saturated fat found in dairy, and in particular fermented dairy such as yoghurt, has less association with raised LDL and, in fact, these foods may be beneficial in reducing your risk of heart disease and stroke.[22]

Public Health England guidelines recommend that we should not be eating more than 31g saturated fat per day for men and 24g for women or less than 22g for children under ten and less than 18g for four- to six-year-olds.[13] However, estimating the amount of fat in our diet is not very practical and it is easier to focus on the *types* of fats we are eating.

Unsaturated or 'good' fats can be split again into monounsaturated or polyunsaturated fats. Although some debate remains, there is good evidence to suggest that replacing saturated fats with unsaturated fats can reduce the risk of heart disease. However, it is important to have a good balance of monounsaturated and polyunsaturated fats as these have different benefits to health.

Foods higher in monounsaturated fats (MUFA) include olive oil, olives, rapeseed oil, avocados and most nuts. Seeds such as pumpkin and sesame seeds are also higher in these fats. A diet higher in MUFA has been linked to higher HDL cholesterol, often termed 'good' cholesterol as this can help to mop up excess cholesterol from the blood vessels. As well as being high in MUFA, these foods are rich in other phytonutrients linked to good health. For example, in a large trial known as Predimed, those following a Mediterranean diet supplemented with olive oil and nuts had a 30% reduction in type-2 diabetes and heart disease compared with those following a low-fat diet.[23]

There are two main types of polyunsaturated fats: omega-3 and omega-6. It is essential to include the right mix of them in your diet as they contain essential fatty acids which must be obtained from the diet and are vital for producing hormones, supporting our immune system, blood clotting and wound healing.

Omega-3 fats are found in oily fish such as salmon, mackerel, sardines, herring and trout. The current advice is to include two portions of fish in our diet per week, one of which should be an oily fish.[24] Vegetarians can convert alpha-linolenic acid (ALA) to the active form of omega-3 from plant-based sources such as flaxseeds, chia seeds, linseed oil, rapeseed oil, walnuts and enriched eggs.[25] There is considerable evidence that omega-3 reduces the risk of heart disease, particularly for those who have pre-existing heart problems.[26]

Omega-6 fats are present mainly in vegetable oils, such as sunflower, corn and soya-bean oil. They are also found in walnuts and pumpkin and sunflower seeds.

All types of fats are high in energy: a single gram of fat provides 9kcal compared with 4kcal per gram for carbohydrates and proteins, so adding extra fat to your diet, regardless of the source, may lead to weight gain.

In summary, cutting down on saturated fats and replacing them with a variety of unsaturated fats is beneficial for our health.

Tips to cut down on saturated fats:

○ Trim all visible fat off meat.
○ Grill, bake or steam food rather than frying or roasting it.
○ Choose lean meat or reduced-fat mince.
○ Measure the oil you use or use a spray or brush rather than pouring it.
○ Use olive oil or rapeseed oil instead of butter, lard or ghee.
○ Switch to skimmed or semi-skimmed milk.
○ Check food labels – processed foods and ready meals can be quite high in fat, salt and sugar. When you can, cook from scratch.

○ Include more oily fish, nuts, olives and avocado in your diet.

Which oils are best for cooking?

Oils play an important role in our diets, and fats, including oils, are important for energy and various body functions. Oils are useful in cooking as they help to carry flavours from other ingredients and are used for frying and other methods of cooking.

Oils change structure when heated, and some are better suited to heating to higher temperatures than others. The 'smoke point' is the temperature at which an oil burns and starts to break down, which directly affects how you use it in the kitchen.

Olive oil, particularly cold-pressed extra-virgin olive oil, is my oil of choice. It is a key component of the Mediterranean diet, made from cold-pressing and extracting oil directly from olives. It is linked to many health benefits, from protecting against heart disease to reducing the risk of type-2 diabetes.[23]

Extra-virgin olive oil also contains numerous polyphenols and nutrients, like vitamin E, giving it additional protective antioxidant properties.[27]

The following are oils I have in my kitchen, with examples of how I like to use them:

○ Extra-virgin olive oil – has a lower smoke point of around 180–190ºC. I use this cold in salads, as a drizzle or in dressings. I also use it for cooking when I can control the temperature to below its smoke point, for traybakes and baking.

○ Rapeseed oil – has a high smoke point. I use this for cooking and frying at high temperatures. I prefer its flavour to extra-virgin olive oil for Indian recipes.
○ Light olive oil – this is extra-virgin olive oil that has been refined using heat to give it a higher smoke point. I use this for cooking when I need to heat the oil to higher temperatures, as for frying, stir-frying and baking. It has fewer nutrients than extra-virgin olive oil, due its refinement.
○ Sesame oil and avocado oil – I use these to add flavour, drizzled on stir-fries, or in dressings.

Protein

Protein is the topic I get asked about most in my clinic: 'How can I eat enough protein?', 'Does my child get enough protein?' and 'What are the best vegetarian sources of protein?'

Protein is a macronutrient that our bodies need for growth and repair, in particular for bones and muscles. It also provides important cellular building blocks, so our protein needs change over the course of our lives. The Reference Nutrient Intake (RNI) is 0.75g protein per kilogram of body weight for average-weight adults.[28] In the UK, the average intake of protein is above this recommendation across all age groups.[20]

However, 0.75g per kg is the level required to avoid deficiency, and optimal protein intake will vary depending on many factors, including age, muscle mass, activity and health. For example, to maintain muscle as we age, our protein requirements increase.[29]

Protein requirements are also higher during critical illness or if recovering from surgery[30] and are higher during pregnancy and when breastfeeding.[28]

Protein needs also vary depending on our physical activity. People who like going for a run or to an exercise class are unlikely to need more protein, but those exercising at a high level may benefit from extra protein after a training session to help muscles rebuild.

Protein is essential for child growth and development, but, reassuringly, UK data suggests that kids are easily meeting the recommended level of protein intake.[20] Foods containing protein should be offered to children twice a day, or three times a day if your child is vegetarian.[31]

Proteins are molecules made up of long chains of amino acids. There are about twenty different amino acids found in plant and animal proteins; nine of these are 'essential amino acids' as they cannot be made by the body and must be provided through diet. Many protein-rich foods are also important sources of micronutrients, such as iron and zinc in meat and calcium and iodine in dairy foods.

Good sources of protein include meat, fish, dairy products, eggs, nuts, soya beans, peas*, lentils*, beans*, amaranth and quinoa.

* *These proteins contain eight of the nine essential amino acids, but it is easy to obtain all nine amino acids by combining them with rice, bread, nuts, seeds or yoghurt; for example, rice and beans, daal and chapati, or hummus and pitta.*

Dietary guidelines are promoting a shift towards getting more protein from plant-based sources rather than from meat, particularly red and processed meats, not just for the nutritional benefit (less saturated fat and increased fibre), but because this is also more environmentally sustainable, supporting planetary health too.[32]

Here are some practical ways to eat more non-meat proteins:

○ Eat protein-rich snacks such as nuts, edamame beans, hummus and cottage cheese.
○ Replace cereal with toast and eggs for breakfast or stir an egg into your porridge.
○ Swap regular yoghurt for Greek (not 'Greek-style') yoghurt.
○ Sprinkle seeds like hemp, pumpkin, sunflower or chia seeds onto foods.
○ Add nut butters to sauces, spread them on toast or bread instead of butter, or blend them into smoothies.
○ Swap refined carbs for whole grains.
○ Try to add some beans to all meals – into curries, blended as dips and tossed into salads.
○ Swap rice or pasta for quinoa or amaranth.
○ Try adding silken tofu to smoothies, sauces or even puddings.
○ Try adding ground almonds instead of flour into bakes.
○ Try adding nutritional yeast to recipes for flavour; this can often replace cheese.

Throughout my book, you will see a lot of recipes putting these suggestions into practice.

Eating the rainbow and 'five a day'

'Eating the rainbow' is a simple and memorable way to encourage a diverse and balanced diet by consuming a wide variety of fruits and vegetables of many different colours. Each colour represents a different type of beneficial nutrient or phytochemical that contributes to overall health.

Generally, each colour in the rainbow has its own nutritional benefit. Colour-associated fruit and veg variety may have additional benefits to health beyond recommendations to increase fruit and veg intake.[33] For example, **red** tomatoes, red peppers, strawberries and watermelons contain lycopene, which may have antioxidant properties and is associated with heart health. **Orange** carrots, sweet potatoes, oranges and mangoes are high in beta-carotene, which the body can convert into vitamin A. They are essential for eye health and immune function and have been linked to reduced risks of heart disease and type-2 diabetes. Leafy **green** vegetables like spinach and kale, broccoli and green beans are rich in vitamins like folate and minerals like iron and calcium. Iron is essential for transporting oxygen around the body and supporting all our organs. Calcium is important for bone health. Blueberries, blackberries and **purple** grapes are packed with antioxidants called anthocyanins, which are linked to improved blood-vessel function and a reduction in inflammation linked to cancer and heart-disease risks. **White** and **brown** vegetables, such as cauliflower, garlic, onions and mushrooms, contain allicin, quercetin and other compounds that may have various health benefits, including immune support, reduced blood pressure and possibly cancer prevention.

By including a variety of colourful fruits and vegetables in your diet, you will ensure you're getting a wide range of nutrients, vitamins and antioxidants.

The five a day recommendation encourages individuals to consume at least five portions of fruit and vegetables every day as part of a healthy diet. Beans and lentils, which are good sources of carbohydrates and protein, but also contain essential vitamins and minerals, count towards your five a day; however, they only count as one portion, regardless of the amount or type you eat. Potatoes *don't* count towards your five a day. The regular consumption of a variety of fruits and vegetables of all colours has been shown to help reduce the risk of chronic diseases like heart disease,[34] type-2 diabetes,[35] and certain types of cancer.[17]

Your five portions a day can be fresh, frozen, dried or even from a tin. A portion size varies depending on the fruit or vegetable. For example, a medium-sized apple or banana, a handful of berries or three heaped tablespoons of cooked vegetables or beans and lentils generally count as one portion. Different colours and types of fruits and vegetables offer different health benefits, so it's best to add as much variety as you can.

Five a day is the minimum, so, ideally, you want to regularly exceed it. Variety is also key, so your five a day shouldn't comprise just fruit, for example.

Practical ways to reach your five a day:

○ Make vegetables and fruit at breakfast the norm! Tomatoes on toast, carrots or fruit in porridge, cucumber sticks for dippy eggs – the possibilities are endless.
○ Add lentils and beans to curries, stews and soups.
○ Swap out half the meat in a recipe for chickpeas or lentils.
○ Add vegetables to rice – frozen peas and sweetcorn are my personal favourites.
○ Snack on fruit with nut butter or vegetable sticks with cottage cheese or hummus.
○ Swap half the potatoes in mash for carrots or swedes – this makes a fantastic pie topping too (see page 59).
○ Try Greek yoghurt and fruit for pudding.
○ Add a simple side salad to your meal – for example lettuce, tomatoes and cucumber.

Plant points

'Plant points' build on the concept of five a day by introducing variety. Basically, you get a plant point for every plant-based food you incorporate in your diet. As a general guide, eating a diet that consists of at least thirty different types of plant points per week can help to ensure you are eating a nutrient-packed diet. Studies have shown that eating this number of different plant foods a week can improve your gut health and gut microbiome.[36] Research has also shown that

ABOVE Chopping vegetables with Kush.

TOP RIGHT Yash sprinkles parsley onto his favourite salad dish.

RIGHT Cooking with my niece, Jaya.

eating more plant-based food can be linked to a reduced risk of raised blood pressure,[37] type-2 diabetes, cardiovascular disease[14] and some cancers.[17]

Plant points refer to any foods that are grown: fruits and vegetables; whole grains (such as oats, whole wheat, quinoa, bulgur, brown rice); legumes (such as beans and pulses); nuts and seeds; and herbs and spices (though each of these counts as only one quarter of a plant point).

A point is awarded for every different plant you eat – not for portion size, because the focus is on variety. So if you eat two red apples that counts as only a single plant point. However, colours are important, so if you ate one red and one green apple, that would count as two plant points. Olive oil, garlic, tea and coffee count as one quarter of a plant point. White bread, white pasta and refined plant foods such as juices do not count as plant points.

Eating thirty different plant points over the course of a week can seem quite daunting, but the points quickly add up. If we look at the very first recipe in this book – Chicken, Leek & Lentil Pie (page 48) – despite it not being a vegetarian recipe, we already have four plant points (lentils, leeks, peas, garlic, olive oil, turmeric and black pepper). Add a simple side salad and that very quickly becomes seven plant points in just one meal! The rest of that day could be porridge with grated carrot, walnuts, hemp seeds, blueberries and cinnamon, with a coffee, for breakfast (5.5 plant points); cashew nuts and an apple as a snack (2 plant points); Miso Noodle Soup (page 98) with tofu, edamame beans, mangetout, spinach and cabbage for lunch (5 plant points).

During a single day, you could easily eat over half the week's thirty plant points. But looking at the week as a whole, you can see that you have a lot of flexibility to get to that magic number of thirty plant points. There might be days when you get only a few plant points, but that's okay. Once again, the focus is on what you can *add* to your diet rather than restricting what you can eat.

All about iron

Iron deficiency is one of the most common nutritional deficiencies I encounter in my clinical practice. Iron is an essential nutrient, meaning our bodies cannot make it and we need to get it from our food. It is essential for various bodily functions, most notably for the production of haemoglobin, a protein found in red blood cells that carries oxygen to tissues throughout the body so that they can function.

The amount of iron your body needs varies depending on your age. Public Health England guidelines[13] are 8.7mg for men aged 19 or over and women aged 50 or over and 14.7mg for women aged 19–49 (or women over the age of 50 who are still menstruating).

Insufficient iron levels can lead to a condition called anaemia, which is characterised by fatigue, weakness, pale skin and difficulty concentrating. If you are worried you may have a deficiency, it is important to see your doctor. Iron deficiency can be due to several factors, including an insufficient intake of iron-rich foods, suboptimal iron absorption within the digestive system or heightened iron demands due to factors such as pregnancy or heavy menstrual bleeding. Consequently, a common question asked by my patients is, 'How do I get enough iron in my diet?'

Fortunately, many foods are rich in iron and there are numerous ways to help to increase iron absorption from our food. If you try to incorporate just a few iron-rich foods into most of your meals, you will easily meet your daily iron requirements.

Iron exists in two forms: haem iron, which is the most easily absorbed by the body and is found in meat; and non-haem iron, which is less easily absorbed by the body and is found in vegetables, beans, pulses and grains.

Good sources of haem iron are liver and red meat (ideally, these should be eaten in moderation) and some fish and shellfish, such as mussels, anchovies and sardines. Poultry contains less iron, so go for cuts such as thighs, which are higher in iron.

Good sources of non-haem iron are eggs; beans, such as edamame beans, kidney beans and chickpeas; nuts; dried foods, such as raisins and apricots; dark green leafy vegetables like spinach and kale; tofu; and fortified cereals (but read the labels carefully as these can be high in sugar and salt).

You can help the body to increase iron absorption by consuming non-haem iron at the same time as haem iron. Vitamin C also increases the absorption of iron from food, while dairy products reduce iron absorption.

Here are some practical ways to increase iron absorption from your meals:

○ Use vegetables rich in vitamin C in your recipe, such as broccoli, peppers, tomatoes, spinach, cauliflower and red cabbage.
○ Add a squeeze of lemon juice at the end of cooking to a curry, daal, soup or stew.
○ Have a side salad containing cucumber, tomatoes and peppers with your meal.
○ Pair your meal with a fruit dessert high in vitamin C, such as kiwi, oranges, strawberries or melon.
○ Avoid dairy products, fizzy drinks, tea and coffee with meals, as they can all reduce the absorption of iron.

Most people should be able to get enough iron through a balanced diet. If you are worried you might not be getting enough iron, please consult a dietitian or doctor.

Vitamin D and calcium

Vitamin D is known as the 'sunshine vitamin' because our skin can produce it only when exposed to daylight, unlike other vitamins, which our bodies cannot produce. So even if you eat a healthy, well-balanced diet that provides all the other nutrients your body needs, it is unlikely to provide you with enough vitamin D.

It's the sun's ultraviolet rays that help you to synthesise vitamin D in your body. You don't have to sunbathe to get enough sun; most people in the UK get sufficient vitamin D from getting sunshine on just their faces and arms for about fifteen minutes a day between 10am and 3pm from April to September (for Caucasian skin).[38] For darker skin types, you need about 25 to 40 minutes of exposure.[39] However, in the UK, during the autumn and winter months (October to early March), there is not enough sunlight for the synthesis of vitamin D in the skin and we rely purely on dietary sources and supplements. The current UK NHS guidelines advise that all adults and children over the age of one in the UK should take 10mg (400 international units) of vitamin D between October and March.[38] These are available over the counter in the UK and are provided free as a part of a multivitamin for pregnant women and children under the age of four if they are eligible (on welfare benefits, for example) via the Healthy Start scheme.[40] For children from six months to five years who are being breastfed or taking less than 500ml fortified formula milk, it is recommended that they take a supplement containing vitamins A, C and D.[41]

There are some groups of people who are at increased risk of not producing enough vitamin D, and they should consider year-round supplementation:

○ People with darker skin tones, as the melanin in their skin affects the body's ability to synthesise vitamin D.
○ People who spend little time outdoors – for example, if you work night shifts, those who are housebound or office workers.
○ Those who are pregnant or breastfeeding.
○ If you cover most of your skin when outside.
○ People over the age of 65, as their skin is not as good at making vitamin D.
○ People living further north in the UK; the further north you live, the less likely it is that the sunlight will be sufficiently strong for your skin to make vitamin D.

Vitamin D is crucial, together with calcium and phosphorus, for the production and maintenance of strong bones, teeth and muscles. Without sufficient vitamin D, even with a diet rich in calcium – such as one with lots of low-fat dairy products and leafy greens – you can't effectively absorb calcium, which is essential for the functions of bones and cells.

Children who do not get enough vitamin D can develop a condition called rickets, which can cause permanent deformities of the bones, weaken muscles and reduce growth. Adults who don't receive adequate vitamin D can develop a condition called osteomalacia, resulting in bone pain and muscle weakness. Vitamin D deficiency remains common in the UK, especially in those with darker skin.[42]

Foods rich in vitamin D include oily fish, such as salmon, sardines, pilchards, trout, herring and kippers; eggs; some margarines; breakfast cereals; infant formula milk; yoghurts fortified with vitamin D; and mushrooms.

Should I take vitamin supplements?

Apart from vitamin D, most people should be able to obtain all the vitamins and minerals they need from a healthy, balanced diet and do not need to take daily vitamin supplements. However, there are certain groups of people who are at increased risk of deficiency and should consider supplements:

○ Pregnant women or those trying to conceive are advised to take 400 micrograms of folic acid until the twelfth week of pregnancy to help prevent neural-tube defects like spina bifida in their unborn child. Anyone at high risk (such as someone with a prior neural-tube defect or with type-1 or type-2 diabetes) should be prescribed 5 milligrams of folic acid per day.[43]

○ Children aged six months to five years should take a supplement containing vitamins A, C and D.[41] You can get these free in the UK if you are eligible, as part of the government's Healthy Start scheme.[40]

○ On the advice of your doctor – some people are diagnosed with deficiencies due to various medical conditions and may be advised to take additional vitamins.

○ Post-menopausal women or elderly people – speak to your doctor if you are concerned.

Apart from the above groups, if you follow the basic principles outlined in this chapter and aim to get as much variety and as many plant-based foods into your diet as possible, you should be able to get all the vitamins and minerals your body needs to thrive.

Probiotics and prebiotics

I am regularly asked by my patients, 'Should I take a probiotic supplement daily?' Or, 'Should I take a probiotic supplement when I take antibiotics?'

Our gut naturally contains trillions of 'friendly' microorganisms, such as bacteria, collectively called the 'gut microbiome'. They aid in digesting our food and perform various other vital functions in our bodies, such as strengthening our immune system. In fact, we are continuously discovering more about our gut microbiome. A less diverse microbiome has been linked to many diseases, including obesity, type-2 diabetes, bowel disorders and several types of cancer.[44,45] However, these friendly bacteria are in constant competition for space in our guts with the 'unfriendly' microorganisms. Therefore, it is essential to strive for a healthy balance of 'friendly' organisms. So, how can you achieve this?

Probiotics are foods that contain these useful microorganisms. Growing up in an Indian household, I had, unknowingly, already been eating and drinking my prebiotics and probiotics as part of a healthy Indian diet. Lassi and fermented Indian pickles, for example, contain probiotic bacteria to support our gut health. In fact, probiotics are a traditional part of many diets across the world – such as kimchi and miso in Asia, sauerkraut in Germany.

With more research emerging every day on the benefits of improving our gut microbiome, you can now find a host of fashionable probiotic drinks such as kombucha and kefir in supermarkets. These can be quite expensive, which begs the question: what should you be taking, and when?

One way we can achieve a balance of good gut organisms may be by consuming fermented food and drinks rich in probiotics.[46] Although we are still lacking evidence from big trials to fine-tune our understanding, the following drinks and foods can support a healthy microbiome, as well as bring other health benefits: live yoghurt; kefir; kombucha; sauerkraut; kimchi; miso; and pickles (in salty water, not vinegar). Independent of the effect on the microbiome, the process of fermentation improves the nutrient profile of the food. For example, lactic acid can convert phytonutrients to a more active form which has been associated with improved heart and immune health.[47]

There is exciting research going on regarding these foods and into the use of probiotic supplements, which contain strains of 'good bacteria' for your gut microbiome.

So, if we already have trillions of good bacteria in our gut, how can we support our existing gut microbiome to keep it healthy? This is where prebiotics come in.

Prebiotics are foods containing fibre that our bodies can't digest; however, they are the perfect 'food' for our friendly gut microbiome, so it is important to incorporate these foods into your diet regularly in order to support your gut. The best way to do this is by incorporating as much variety, especially with regard to fruits and vegetables (back to plant points again), in your diet as possible.

Good sources of prebiotics include vegetables such as asparagus, onions, leeks, Jerusalem artichokes and garlic; fruits such as bananas, apples, blueberries and pears; whole grains such as barley, wheat, rye and oats; nuts and seeds, such as almonds and flaxseeds; legumes and beans; soy, such as tofu and miso.

Common items from the list above feature heavily in my recipes, allowing you to easily make prebiotics a part of your everyday meals. Once again, we are focusing here on what we can *add* to our diets rather than restricting certain foods.

So are there any times when probiotic supplements may be useful? Probiotic supplements are usually drinks that contain lots of friendly gut bacteria, but they need to be taken daily as they don't colonise the gut. They also tend to be quite expensive.

There are times in your life when you might have an imbalance in your body's own friendly gut microbiome: when you have a serious diarrhoeal illness or when you are taking antibiotics, which help to fight a bacterial infection, but also kill some of your body's own gut microbiome. In both these cases, there is evidence to show that increasing your intake of probiotics via probiotic food, drinks or supplements, or both, may help if you take them as soon as you start the antibiotics and continue for at least one week after the end of the course. The British Dietetic Association has produced a leaflet on other conditions where probiotics may be trialled. These include reducing travellers' diarrhoea, and as a treatment for constipation and some bowel disorders, including irritable bowel syndrome (IBS), Crohn's disease and colitis.[48]

In our family, our favourite way to up our intake of probiotics and prebiotics is via this bonus recipe opposite – my favourite pre- and probiotic smoothie.

Probiotic & Prebiotic Smoothie

This smoothie is the perfect way to start the day and is very family friendly. It is packed with pre- and probiotics to keep your gut healthy and happy. My youngest likes to add blueberries to his to 'make it purple', but you can add your favourite berries if you prefer. I take mine to work to drink at my desk.

You can even prepare the smoothie and leave it overnight in the fridge (minus the banana). The oats become softer and easier to blend if they have been soaked – and the smoothie tastes even better!

SERVES 2

1 banana

25g porridge oats

100g silken tofu

100g live yoghurt or kefir

2 tbsp ground almonds

1 tbsp hemp hearts

1 tsp cacao powder

250ml milk of choice

Blend all the ingredients in a blender until you have a thick smoothie. Add a little more milk as needed to adjust the consistency and enjoy right away!

Vegan, vegetarian and plant-based diets

The decision to adopt a vegetarian or vegan diet is often influenced by a growing awareness of how our food choices impact not only our health but also the environment and animal welfare.

When evaluating the healthiness of vegetarian or vegan diets, it's crucial to consider several factors. First and foremost, the quality of any diet, regardless of whether it is vegetarian or not, is key. A well-planned vegetarian or vegan diet can be incredibly nutritious, packed with essential vitamins, minerals, fibre and antioxidants. Studies have suggested that such diets can be associated with lower risks of chronic diseases, such as heart disease, diabetes and certain cancers.[49] Yet, the inherent healthiness of these diets doesn't mean they are automatically superior. For example, many vegan or vegetarian meat alternatives can be heavily processed and contain many additives with minimal nutritional benefits. A vegetarian diet that lacks other important elements of a healthy diet can be detrimental to health, just as an unbalanced omnivorous diet can be.

For vegetarians or vegans, proper dietary planning is essential to ensure they receive all the nutrients they need. This includes paying attention to sources of protein, iron, vitamin B12, calcium and omega-3 fatty acids, which are often more abundant in animal-based foods. Fortunately, these nutrients can be obtained through careful dietary choices or, if need be, from supplements. It's also important to recognise that the health benefits associated with vegetarian or vegan diets can be derived not only from the absence of meat, but also from the increased consumption of whole, plant-based foods.

Whether one opts for a vegetarian, vegan or omnivorous diet, the emphasis should always be on consuming a wide variety of nutrient-dense, minimally processed foods, along with a conscientious consideration of individual nutritional needs. Ultimately, the path to a healthy diet is shaped by informed choices and an understanding of the broader implications of one's food choices on personal health, animal welfare and the planet, taking into account individual circumstances and constraints.

Tips for following a vegetarian or vegan diet:

○ Eat at least five portions of fruit or vegetables a day.
○ Maximise your plant points to above 30 a week.
○ Milk and dairy products are good sources of protein, calcium, iodine and vitamins A and B12. If you are vegan, opt for fortified alternatives.
○ Eat a variety of protein sources to get the right mixture of amino acids; for example, tofu, tempeh, beans, peas, lentils and eggs.
○ Focus on iron-rich foods.
○ Add vitamin B12-rich foods such as milk, cheese or eggs, or fortified products like Marmite, nutritional yeast and fortified cereals.
○ Add vegetarian sources of omega-3, for example, flaxseeds, rapeseed oil, walnuts and enriched eggs.

In this book, I have suggested a vegetarian or vegan alternative for every recipe, except in the Meat-free chapter, which are all, of course, meat-free!

Salt

Whilst our bodies do need small amounts of sodium to conduct nerve impulses, contract and relax muscles and maintain the proper balance of water and minerals, eating too much salt is linked to raised blood pressure, which can increase the risk of heart attacks and strokes, whereas reducing salt along with a diet rich in fruit and vegetables helps to lower blood pressure.[37] It has also been linked to stomach cancer,[50] and may be linked to increased risks for osteoporosis.[51]

The recommended daily amount of salt for adults (11 years and over) is less than 6g per person. This is the equivalent of 1 teaspoon per day. That includes salt that is naturally present in the food as well as the salt that is added after cooking. For children, this is a lot lower. Most people in the UK eat far too much salt. Public Health England guidelines[13] for maximum recommended salt intake are: 7 to 10 years – no more than 5g; 4 to 6 years – no more than 3g; 1 to 3 years – no more than 2g; under 1 year – less than 1g.

The recipes in my book suggest adding only small amounts of salt, because I try to enhance flavour with herbs and spices instead of salt. If you normally use a large amount of salt, it is not easy to drastically reduce your salt intake. After all, food is for enjoyment as well as nutrition. My recipe suggestions are a guide to aim for; it might be easier to start by slightly reducing the amount of salt you use each week until you become accustomed to using smaller amounts.

Tips to reduce salt:

○ Try halving the salt in your usual recipe and add a little lemon juice, chilli, herbs or spices for more flavour.
○ Don't put table salt on the dining table, but do bring the pepper grinder and/or some chilli flakes for flavour.
○ Don't add any additional salt to young children's food, so they become accustomed to flavours in foods without salt. Babies shouldn't have any added salt as their kidneys cannot process it.
○ Check labels on any ready-made food you buy for salt content – bread and breakfast cereals can be surprisingly high in salt!
○ Try low-salt alternatives, such as reduced-salt soy sauce and stock cubes.
○ Always buy tinned vegetables and pulses in water with no added salt or sugar.
○ Reduce your intake of salty foods such as cured or processed meats like ham and bacon, smoked salmon, cheese and pickles.
○ Try unsalted nuts and crackers or rice cakes for snacks.
○ Try to avoid ready-made sauces as they can be high in salt. If possible, make your own.
○ Condiments, such as ketchup, chilli and sweet sauces, can be very high in salt, so use them in moderation, or why not make your own?

Ultra-processed foods

Ultra-processed foods, or UPFs, are foods that have been changed significantly from their original state through processing. They are generally high in saturated fats, sugar and salt and lower in fibre, vitamins and minerals with other additives such as flavourings, preservatives and emulsifiers. As discussed, links between excess consumption of saturated fat, sugars and salt and poorer health outcomes are well established. UPFs are manufactured to improve palatability which encourages us to overeat foods that have been stripped of other beneficial nutrients. Diets high in UPFs have been linked to increased risks for many health conditions including heart disease, obesity, bowel disorders, some cancers and depression.[52,53]

Unfortunately, the UK is one of the biggest consumers of UPFs in Europe.[54] Lower costs, ease of manufacture and the need for a long shelf life all drive industries to produce more and more of these types of foods.

In an ideal world, all our food would come directly from the farm to our plates, but this isn't practical, convenient or cost-effective for most people. A lot of our food does undergo some sort of processing to give it a longer life and to make it more palatable, and not all these foods are detrimental to our health. To avoid UPFs but still enjoy the convenience of minimally processed foods without an adverse effect on our health, we need a better understanding of the different kinds of processed foods.

The NOVA classification system,[55] designed by an international group of food scientists and researchers, splits foods into four main categories.

Group 1 includes unprocessed or minimally processed foods in their natural state, such as meat, vegetables, eggs, nuts and seeds. They can be animal or plant foods that may have undergone minimal processing to make them edible, such as cooking, drying or freezing. Or they may have undergone a process to make them safer to eat, such as pasteurising milk.

Group 2 includes processed ingredients, such as oils, butter, sugar and salt, which wouldn't be eaten alone but are used with unprocessed natural foods.

Group 3 includes processed foods that are usually a combination of the above two groups that have been combined, prepared and then packaged to make them taste better or last longer. Whilst these foods have been altered, it's usually not in a way that may be detrimental to your health. Examples of these include tinned fruits and vegetables, cheese, tofu and tinned fish.

Group 4 are ultra-processed foods, those that have often undergone multiple processing stages and have had ingredients added. They usually contain few or no ingredients from the first group. When products made from Group 1 or Group 3 products contain any cosmetic or sensory intensifying additives, such as food colourings or artificial sweeteners, they are classified in Group 4. Examples of these types of foods include fizzy drinks;

packaged snacks such as sweets and crisps; breakfast cereals; mass-produced pastries, bread and cakes; margarine and other spreads; vegan meat and cheese alternatives; ready-to-eat meals, such as pies, burgers and chicken nuggets.

If all UPFs are unhealthy, then why not just cut all UPFs from our diet? It's not quite that simple. Let's take a closer look at Group 4. Heavily processed meat, biscuits and confectionery would be in this category, in addition to whole-grain breads and cereals or a tin of baked beans. However, ultra-processed meats are high in saturated fats and salt and are linked to an increased risk of heart disease, strokes and some cancers.[52, 53] Whereas whole-grain cereal, bread or baked beans can be nutritious and form part of a balanced diet to help people to reach their macro- and micronutrient goals and are linked to health benefits.[8,9,14,17,19]

Due to the widespread availability and convenience of highly processed foods, most of us may incorporate them into our diets from time to time. However, consuming them infrequently, rather than regularly, as part of a diverse, nutritious and well-balanced diet is unlikely to pose a long-term health risk. My aim is to support you with easy, family-friendly recipes to help replace UPFs with convenient, freshly prepared meals designed to maximise flavour, increase nutrient density and reduce additives, saturated fat, sugar and salt.

Here are some practical ways to reduce UPFs in your diet:

○ Cook from scratch whenever you can, using raw ingredients.
○ Try to avoid ready-made sauces or burgers, which often contain a lot of additives.
○ Batch-cooking, of just sauces or whole meals, can make life a lot easier.
○ Batch-cook ingredients like brown rice that might take longer to cook and freeze portions for when you need a meal quickly. When freezing rice, it is important to let it cool quickly to room temperature, then freeze it right away once cold to prevent the growth of harmful bacteria that can cause food poisoning. For the same reason, rice must be reheated until it is completely heated through and piping hot.
○ Batch-prepare ingredients you use regularly. For example, garlic and ginger can be peeled and minced in bulk and frozen in portions.
○ Read ingredient labels carefully and try to choose products with the smallest quantities of additives.

Budget, culture and healthy food

Not everyone has equal access to the resources and options needed to adopt a particular type of diet. Budget constraints can limit the choices available. Geographic location can also play a role; access to a wide variety of fresh fruits, vegetables and plant-based protein sources may be more limited in some areas. Additionally, cultural beliefs, traditions and religion all play an important role in people's diets.

Whilst I have done my best to make most of my recipes as accessible as possible, a limited budget can play a significant role in someone's diet. Whilst cooking from scratch is often cheaper than a ready-meal or a takeaway, it does require an initial investment in the raw ingredients and spices. For example, a ready-made supermarket pizza can be purchased for less than the cost of the raw ingredients needed to make a lentil curry and rice, and is also easier to prepare.

We know that cooking from scratch has a significant positive effect on our mental health and well-being that goes well beyond simply providing nutrition.[56]

Whilst this is not a 'budget' cookbook, I have tried to include seasonal swaps and ways to reduce the cost of recipes. If you are cooking on a budget, I have a free downloadable eBook on my website (drchintalskitchen.com) with easy, healthy 50p recipes.

Here are some ways to reduce the cost of healthy eating:

○ With meat, focus on quality not quantity. Buy the best you can afford, but use less of it. Swap out half of the meat in a recipe for a cheaper alternative such as chickpeas or lentils. Or swap out the meat completely – see my Meat-free Monday chapter and all the vegetarian alternatives offered throughout the book.
○ Buy cheaper cuts of meat. Chicken thighs or legs are a lot cheaper than

boneless breast pieces. Often buying a whole chicken or cuts with the bone in and portioning it yourself can be cheaper, and the bones can make a nutritious bone broth or stock. Chicken cooked on the bone is always so much more tender too.

○ Add a tin of beans or lentils to any meal to make it go further.

○ Try to plan your meals so you can use up all your ingredients and avoid food waste. Sometimes doubling up on a recipe may be more cost-effective.

○ Make extra and take leftovers for lunch! Not only do leftovers taste better but they are definitely cheaper than buying a sandwich or something else at work.

○ Frozen and tinned vegetables are often cheaper than fresh vegetables and just as nutritious. (Buy tinned foods in their own juice or water without added salt or sugar.)

○ Eat seasonally – seasonal fruits and vegetables will often be cheaper. Supermarkets in the UK always have special prices for these weekly – try to buy these when you can and use them to swap into recipes.

○ If you have a freezer, use it! Buy food in bulk when on offer and freeze it. Make double or batch-cook and freeze meals to save time and money.

○ If you have space, try to buy pantry staples with a long shelf life when on sale, for example, rice, pasta and other whole grains, tinned beans and pulses, dried lentils and so on.

○ Try tinned fish as an alternative to fresh fish – tinned sardines, for example. Tinned salmon often contains edible bones, which are good sources of calcium. Tinned salmon, pilchards, sardines and mackerel are oily fish, which we are advised to eat once a week.

○ Try energy-efficient cooking devices such as slow cookers, microwaves, pressure cookers and air fryers. If you are turning the oven on, make the most of it. For example, roast some extra vegetables to use another day. If using the hob, use the smallest pan needed and pop on a lid to preserve heat and speed up the cooking time.

○ Peanuts, sunflower seeds and pumpkin seeds are super nutritious and cheaper than other nuts and seeds for snacks.

○ Avoid food waste – leftover veggies can be repurposed into soups or stir-fries. Freeze anything left over to preserve it for up to three months. For example, if you buy a large loaf of bread, slice it and freeze it, then remove slices as you need them. Use vegetable peelings and animal bones to make stock.

○ Make your own snacks, such as popcorn and hummus. They are so much cheaper to make at home and you can control the amount of salt, sugar and oil they contain.

The building blocks for a 'healthy plate'

How do you build a healthy, balanced diet in practice? The key word is balance. Even some UPFs can be nutritious and convenient as part of a balanced diet.

In the UK, the Eatwell Guide[24] visually represents various food and beverage categories and shows us how much of what we eat should come from each food group to achieve a healthy, balanced diet. Although depicted as a plate, it is not a suggestion for what should be on your plate for every meal, but more of a guide to eating well over the course of a day or a week. The general principles are:

○ To eat five or more portions of fruit and vegetables a day. This should form at least one-third of our food for the day.
○ Starchy food should make up just over one-third of the food we eat. Choose whole carbs and whole grains over refined carbs.
○ Eat some beans, pulses, fish, eggs, meat and other protein foods. Choose lean cuts of meat and mince and eat less red and processed meat. Aim for at least two portions (2 x 140g) of fish every week, one of which should be oily, such as salmon, sardines or mackerel.
○ Have some dairy or dairy alternatives (such as soya drinks and yoghurts fortified with calcium and B vitamins).

○ Choose unsaturated oils and spreads and eat these in small amounts.
○ Eat foods high in fat, salt and sugar less often and in small amounts.
○ Drink plenty of fluids – the UK NHS guidelines recommends six to eight cups or glasses a day.

The second half of my book focuses on putting a lot of these principles into practice in the kitchen. I thought it might be helpful to look at how I put some of the Eatwell Guide into practice practically in terms of designing my meals per plate.

I base most of my meals and recipes around a few basic principles:

○ I split the plate so that half of it contains vegetables, at least two different types and colours per meal. The other half is split equally into two quarters, one (mostly whole) carbohydrates, such as brown rice, bulgur or quinoa, while the other quarter is protein, such as chicken, oily fish or tofu.
○ I mostly use olive or rapeseed oil in my cooking.

NOTE
The Eatwell Guide is not applicable to children below the age of two due to their distinct nutritional requirements. For children aged two to five, it is recommended that they transition gradually to consuming the same foods as the rest of the family, following the suggested proportions outlined in the Eatwell Guide.

Opposite is an example of how this might look in practice on your dinner plate if we take the first recipe in this book:

Chicken, Leek & Lentil Pie
1 Vegetables – leeks, garlic, peas, tomatoes and lettuce.
2 Carbohydrates – lentils and filo pastry.
3 Protein – chicken and lentils.
4 Fats – olive oil used in cooking.

Plant points: 7

As always, throughout this chapter and this book, my focus remains on how I can increase the variety of fruits, vegetables and plant-based foods on our families' plates.

Conclusion

This is only a brief overview, designed to give you some food for thought (pun intended!).

To summarise: eat everything in moderation and focus on adding as much variety as you can to your diet. Good health as a result of optimum nutrition will naturally follow. Most importantly, enjoy your food! A healthy diet should not come at the expense of a healthy relationship with food. Food is there for enjoyment as well as nourishment. If you really don't like kale or *açaí*, don't eat kale or *açaí*. There are no one or two superfoods you *must* eat; the balance and variety of foods you enjoy will form a healthy diet and a healthy relationship with food.

There's also more to food than just nutrition; there's the social aspect of eating together, and cooking can be a wonderful mindful activity for some. What there definitely isn't is a 'one-size-fits-all' answer. Your genetics, environmental factors, socio-economic background and budget all play a role. Take from this chapter what works for you and those around you. Make small, sustainable, long-term changes over a time frame that feels right for you and keeps you and your family happy. Rome wasn't built in a day. Extreme, faddish diets are exactly that: extreme fads. They may help with short-term weight-loss goals, but they may not provide all the nutrients your body needs and people often find that the weight they've lost returns just as soon as they revert to their 'normal' way of eating. I once read something that has stuck in my head ever since: 'Measure the success of a diet on health gain, not weight loss.'

Finally, I would say avoid totally restricting foods you enjoy; the only foods you need to avoid are those you really don't like (although, sometimes even those can taste a bit better after a few attempts); those you are allergic to; or those you have been told to avoid by a medical professional due to an illness.

Now, let's move on to the fun part of my book and get cooking!

OPPOSITE Chicken, Leek & Lentil Pie, with a side salad.

My Kitchen Staples

For me, stocking up with pantry staples ensures that I have lots of nutritious ingredients to hand in the kitchen. That way, I always have easy meals at my fingertips, even if my fridge is looking empty. I've split this into three sections to make it easier to digest (excuse the pun!). This is your practical guide to stocking your kitchen so that you have everything on hand to create easy, nutritious meals for you and your family.

1 **Store-cupboard/pantry staples** – my go-to tins, jars and grains for completing meals.
2 **Fill your freezer!** – how I keep my freezer stocked with ingredients and homemade 'ready-meals'.
3 **Spice it up!** – how to spice up your meals with my special seven everyday spices.

Store-cupboard/pantry staples

In today's busy world, when we don't always have the time to make everything from scratch, sometimes convenience is essential. Personally, I don't demonise any foods. All foods feature in my pantry and not every meal is made from scratch, because that's just not practical – and that's okay. I don't beat myself up over it, just as long as *most* of my meals are easy to prepare and can be made from scratch.

For example, a jar of pesto may be seen as a 'processed food'. However, I would argue that using a ready-made jar of pesto, instead of making your own, may leave you time to roast or chop some extra vegetables to stir into the pasta sauce. The resulting pasta with pesto and roast vegetables will

definitely be a more nutritious meal than homemade pasta with pesto without any added vegetables. On a day when I have more time, I love making my own pesto (you can find a super-easy version in the 15-minute Meals chapter, page 90).

The more new foods and variety you can add to your meals, rather than restricting or removing foods, the more nutritious your meals will become. Bearing that in mind, below is a list of some of my pantry staples. Most of these are long-life products, so you can stock up or buy in bulk. I am a total sucker for a BOGOF deal!

The list may look long, but don't be alarmed; it's very likely you have a lot of these ingredients already, and I really have included everything, right down to salt and pepper! If you don't have many of the items on my list, don't worry. I'm not suggesting you go and spend lots of money on pantry ingredients you may not use. Slowly add different items as you try recipes throughout this book and don't re-stock other items that might become redundant as you diversify your meals.

My pantry staples:
- *Pasta* – wholewheat and white (I like to mix it up) and a few different shapes, including spaghetti, linguine and orzo!
- *Rice* – I have brown and white basmati depending on my mood, plus some wild rice for when I'm feeling extra fancy.
- *Grains* – oats, quinoa, bulgur, cornmeal and couscous.
- *Flours* – plain flour, self-raising flour, wholemeal flour and bread flour.
- *Dried pulses* – I usually have red lentils

LEFT Store-cupboard staples in my kitchen.

(essential!), yellow split peas, mung daal and black lentils, as I make a lot of different daal recipes.

○ *Tinned pulses* – kidney beans, chickpeas, butter beans, mixed beans and lentils.
○ *Tinned vegetables* – sweetcorn, spinach, beansprouts and chopped tomatoes.
○ *Tomato purée* and *passata*.
○ *Tinned fruit* – pineapple is so much more cost-effective tinned.
○ *Nuts* – as much variety as possible. I have cashew nuts, almonds, walnuts, pistachios, pecans, ground almonds and flaked almonds.
○ *Seeds* – hemp hearts, linseeds, pumpkin, sunflower and chia seeds.
○ *Oils* – extra-virgin olive oil, light olive oil, rapeseed oil and sesame oil.
○ *Ready-made items* – for example, jars of pesto, harissa, Thai curry paste and hoisin sauce.
○ *Seasoning* – salt, pepper, spices, soy sauce, low-salt vegetable and/or chicken stock cubes and chilli flakes.

Fill your freezer!

My freezer is my backup for everything. And when I say everything, I really do mean everything. When I run out of fruit, there's a stash of berries or bananas in the freezer. If there are no fresh vegetables in the fridge, you can guarantee there is a selection in my freezer. Did you know that most fruit and vegetables we buy in the stores are picked and frozen within a day or two? Therefore, the frozen options are often 'fresher' and contain more nutrients than a vegetable that may have been sitting on a supermarket shelf for a few days and then in your fridge for the next week! In fact, I make a point of freezing any vegetables that have been in my fridge for more than a few days, to preserve their nutrients.

I follow a very simple routine to keep my freezer stocked; if I see that items are almost finished, I simply add them to my weekly shop. Freezer food has a long shelf life, so even if my fridge is empty, I know I will always have a backup in the freezer.

My freezer staple ingredients are:
○ *Frozen berries* – blueberries and raspberries, which are also much cheaper frozen and are perfect for using in smoothies, in bakes or for topping a bowl of porridge or granola.
○ *Other frozen fruit* – mango, melon and banana all freeze well.
○ *Frozen vegetables* – my staples are edamame beans (in pods for snacks, shelled for meals), petit pois, sweetcorn, spinach (chopped and whole leaf), green beans, cauliflower and broccoli.
○ *Other frozen vegetables* – if you're short on time, you can buy pre-diced onions, chopped peppers, sliced mushrooms to make life easier.
○ *Minced garlic and ginger* – I usually peel garlic and ginger in bulk, mince it up and freeze it flat in silicone bags, so you can snap off however much you need. Or

I freeze 1-teaspoon portions in an ice-cube tray.

- *Frozen chillies* – you can grate these straight from frozen to use in a recipe.
- *Frozen herbs* – expensive herbs such as curry leaves, makrut lime leaves and lemongrass often come in quite large packets and you only need a few at a time, so freeze any extra herbs.
- *Chicken* – already cut into cubes or otherwise portioned up for ease.
- *Salmon fillets* – individually frozen so I can take one out as needed for lunch or a quick meal.
- *Cheese* – did you know cheese keeps really well in the freezer and you can use it directly from frozen? I buy a large block as it's more economical, then grate it all and freeze it in a silicone bag. As it's grated, it's easy to remove just what you need for a dish.

I also have a drawer in my freezer dedicated to 'homemade ready-made items'.

- *Homemade 'ready-meals'* – if I'm cooking any meals that allow me to double up and freeze an extra portion, I will. 'Cook once, eat (at least) twice' is my motto! If making a lasagne, I will make an extra tray for the freezer. If making pesto or another sauce, I will make double and freeze a portion. Curries freeze well and taste even better when you use them as the flavour intensifies. My 'ready-meals' can be whipped out the night before and left in the fridge or popped straight into the oven when I get home from work.
- *Pre-made sauces* – this can make whipping up a meal so much easier. If I'm making red pasta or curry sauce, I will make double and freeze half for another day.
- *Freeze leftovers!* I don't mind eating the same meal a couple of days in a row, but three days is pushing it for me, so I simply freeze any leftovers. They are handy for lunchboxes or when you need a meal in a hurry.
- *Freeze cooked rice*, especially brown rice. One thing that often puts me off using brown rice is the amount of time it takes to cook, so my cook's tip is to make a few portions in one go and freeze some so it's ready when you need it (please see note on page 35).
- *Ice cream!* I love ice cream. I was recently given an ice cream maker and I love it. Dark chocolate sorbet is my favourite flavour.

My top tip for the freezer is to make sure you label everything! Trust me, I've learnt the hard way and ended up with coriander-chutney pasta and dipping my pakora in pesto!

By always keeping my freezer well stocked, if I haven't had time to get to the shops, rather than reaching for a takeaway menu, I know I'll be able to whip out a homemade 'ready-meal' or prepared ingredients to allow me to make a speedy meal.

Spice it up!

I love spices! I have so many of them in my kitchen, from all over the world. I love experimenting with them in my cooking, but the truth is, you don't need a drawer full of spices to start using them. My love of spices stems from childhood, growing up in an Indian household where adding many spices to meals was the norm.

Spices are often thought of in terms of heat or chillies, but in reality most spices are meant to enhance flavour rather than add heat. I often speak to parents who are confused regarding spices and avoid using them in their children's meals, often leaving them out of recipes entirely. In Indian culture, even babies are introduced to spices early, often during the initial stages of weaning. A traditional Indian first food is *khichdi*, a nutritious dish containing cumin and turmeric. My mum not only used spices in her cooking, they were also the solution to any ailment I had. If I fell over and hurt my knee, turmeric was instantly applied to the graze rather than a plaster; golden turmeric milk (now fashionably called a turmeric latte) was the cure for all coughs and colds; and meals were always followed by fennel seeds to aid digestion.

However, if I'm honest, whilst I make a conscious effort to use the huge array of spices I hoard in my kitchen spice drawer, the top seven spices in my trusty *masala dabba* are still the most used and restocked spices in my kitchen. So, if you are new to using spices, then my top seven are a great starting point. (I'm going to assume everyone has black pepper so I can sneak an extra spice onto the list!) They will add so much flavour and depth to your meals, I promise you, you won't regret it! I also promise you that we will use every one of the spices below many times throughout this book, because I hate it when a recipe calls for a weird and wonderful spice that is used once and then sits in the spice drawer for months on end, only to end up losing its flavour and being wasted. I'm all about no food waste!

I'll also let you into a little secret: there is no need to buy spice blends. I used to buy all sorts of blends, from garam masala to fajita mix, but I've learnt that it's just as easy to make your own. They always taste better, the aroma is fresher and it means you get to make use of that fancy pestle and mortar you bought for show in the kitchen!

I also tend to buy a lot of whole spices rather than the powdered versions, which will often lose their flavour very quickly even when stored in an airtight jar. The magic happens when you lightly toast whole spices on a medium heat, this draws out the flavour and your kitchen will be filled with the most beautiful aroma. Toasting the spices also makes them much easier to grind into a powder with a simple pestle and mortar or spice grinder.

My essential seven spices are:
1. cumin seeds
2. cardamom pods – both black and green
3. turmeric powder
4. coriander seeds
5. Kashmiri chilli powder*
6. cinnamon sticks (*and* ground cinnamon, as cinnamon is a bit more difficult to grind by hand)
7. smoked paprika

* Kashmiri chilli powder adds a beautiful flavour and colour without too much heat. But if you like chillies and heat you can substitute normal chilli powder.

Most of the recipes in my book incorporate spices. Not only are you adding diversity and additional plant points, you're also diversifying your family's tastes. For me, that's important as I love eating out and travelling. So I know our choice won't be limited when we are in a restaurant, or in a foreign country.

Sunday evening prep

I know this probably sounds like a total pain – after all, Sunday is the day of rest – but hear me out. A little prep on a Sunday (and I mean very little) will save you many hours during the week and I promise that it will definitely stop you ordering a takeaway or reaching for a ready-meal at least once during that week! If you get a food delivery, arrange it for a Sunday (or another day when you are home if you work shifts/ weekends).

I start by washing *all* the fruit and veg for the week ahead before placing it in the fridge. This is much easier than it sounds. Anything that needs a little scrub is first scrubbed and rinsed, then everything goes into a clean sink straight from the shopping bags. I fill the sink with cold water and a cup of white vinegar and leave the fruit and vegetables to soak for about fifteen minutes. Next, I rinse the fruit and vegetables and lay them out on clean tea-towels to dry, turning them over after a bit so they are fully dry. I have smaller boxes inside the drawers in my

fridge, which I line with clean paper towel before placing all the fruit and vegetables directly into the individual sections. Then when someone wants a snack during the week, it's easily accessible, washed and ready to eat, and when I need ingredients for a recipe they are ready to go!

There are a few exceptions to this. Berries and grapes go into a kitchen paper-lined, airtight container and any fruit that will last out of the fridge goes into the fruit bowl for easy access. During the summer, though, most of my fruit is kept in the fridge to keep it fresh.

The second thing I do on a Sunday is to roast a tray or two of my favourite vegetables. This could be as simple as using up all the old produce to make room for the new food delivery, or it could be specifically chosen vegetables. It takes very little effort or time. I roughly chop the vegetables, drizzle them with olive oil, add salt and pepper and roast in large trays at 200ºC, 180ºC fan, gas mark 6 for twenty or so minutes until they are cooked. These vegetables are used for the next few days as sides for a main dish, mixed into salads, rolled into wraps or added to a frittata for a nutritious lunch. This simple meal prep means that I always have some vegetables handy for the beginning of the week. If I'm really stuck, grabbing one of my ready-made curry sauces, a tin of chickpeas and some roasted vegetables makes a delicious, nutritious, easy meal the whole family will love!

Everyday Meals

Welcome to a selection of my easy, mostly quick, everyday meals. Within this collection you'll discover an abundance of one-pan wonders and simple recipes that never compromise on flavour. Enjoy the convenience of preparing quick and easy dishes without sacrificing on taste!

Growing up, my diet predominantly consisted of Indian food, but as we gather around the dinner table at home, we enjoy the diversity of flavours from all corners of the world. Inspired by my parents' culinary experiments, we often enjoyed dishes infused with an Indian twist or transformed into savoury *shaks* (curries) to pair with rice or roti. Through my journey from university to marriage, I was always exploring recipes from various cuisines, experimenting along the way. During my children's weaning journey, I enjoyed exposing them to the array of foods I had now experienced. Interestingly, whilst Indian food has a special place in their hearts, Japanese cuisine holds their ultimate affection!

Although my recipes now span diverse cultures, the 'Indian twist' continues to lovingly find its way, predominantly through the use of spices. To me, recipes are a mere guide, meant to be reinvented and personalised. Feel free to add your own creative touch, and if you do, I'd be thrilled if you shared it with me – I can't wait to see your unique culinary creations!

Chicken, Leek & Lentil Pie

If a meal could give you the warmest hug, this pie is it. It's a balanced, nutritious recipe that comes together in one pan, making it an easy midweek meal option. As I mentioned in my first chapter, reducing the amount of meat in a recipe by using lentils or beans is a great way to cut costs and add more plant points.

SERVES 4–6

2 tbsp olive oil

500g leeks, chopped

1 tsp salt

300g chicken thighs or breasts, cut into small cubes

4 cloves garlic, peeled

1 tsp black pepper

1 x 400g tin of green lentils, drained

200g frozen peas or sweetcorn

3 tbsp plain flour

350ml milk

125g filo pastry

Pinch of turmeric (optional)

COOK'S TIP

Stir a pinch of turmeric into the oil you use to brush the pastry to add colour.

1 Preheat the oven to 200°C, 180°C fan, gas mark 6.

2 Heat 1 tablespoon of the oil in a large ovenproof pan over medium heat. Add the leeks and salt. After a few minutes, once they have softened, add the chicken, garlic and pepper.

3 When the chicken starts to brown (this will take a few minutes), add the lentils, frozen peas or sweetcorn, flour and milk. Stir well to incorporate. This will slowly thicken to form a white sauce. At this point, remove the pan from the heat.

4 Roughly scrunch up each filo sheet and place it gently over the chicken and vegetables. Continue until the whole pie is covered.

5 Brush the filo with the remaining 1 tablespoon of olive oil. Bake for 20 minutes until the pastry turns crisp and golden.

6 Serve right away, as is or with a side salad.

Make it vegetarian
Swap out the chicken for halloumi or tofu in step 2, or use any seasonal vegetables such as broccoli and/or mushrooms.

'If a meal could give you the warmest hug, this pie is it!'

Prawn Bulgur Pilaf

You might recall bulgur from the introductory nutrition chapter. It's a fantastic whole-grain alternative to rice that you can use in numerous dishes, and it makes this one-pan bulgur pilaf an excellent, quick weeknight meal. Feel free to substitute the vegetables with whatever is in season and use halloumi, beans or lentils as the protein source instead of prawns.

SERVES 4

200g bulgur wheat

1 tbsp olive oil

3 green cardamom pods

1 tsp cumin seeds

1 red onion, chopped

4 cloves garlic, chopped

2 different-coloured peppers, deseeded and chopped

100g tomato purée

1 x 400g tin of kidney beans, drained

200g raw shelled king prawns

1 tsp turmeric

1 tsp ground coriander

1 tsp salt

400ml boiling water

200g baby spinach leaves

1 tsp chilli flakes (optional)

1 Rinse and drain the bulgur wheat.

2 In a pan over medium heat, add the oil, cardamom and cumin. Cook for about a minute to release their flavours, then add the chopped onion. Cook the onion until it turns translucent and starts to brown.

3 Add the chopped peppers and cook until they begin to soften – this will take a couple of minutes, then stir in the tomato purée.

4 Next, add the beans, prawns, turmeric, ground coriander, salt and drained bulgur to the pan and mix well. Add the 400ml boiling water, then stir everything well and bring the mixture to a simmer.

5 Finally, scatter the baby spinach leaves over the top and cover the pan with a heavy lid. Cook, covered, over medium heat for 10 minutes. After this time, remove the pan from the heat and leave it covered for an additional 5 minutes.

6 Uncover the pan, stir the spinach leaves into the bulgur and serve immediately with a sprinkle of chilli flakes, if you like.

Make it vegetarian
Use 250g halloumi or 1 x 400g tin of beans or lentils instead of prawns. Add them to the dish in step 4.

Fish Tacos with Mango Salsa

This is an easy fish taco recipe for a midweek meal. I've used salmon as it's a great source of omega-3 heart-healthy fats, but you can switch it up for any firm white fish. My top tip would be to make extra of the Cajun-spice seasoning here to store for later, as I use it frequently throughout the book. There really is no need to buy expensive spice blends and mixes if you can make your own using my top seven spices (see page 44) and a few herbs. If you don't have thyme or oregano in your cupboard, use mixed dried herbs instead.

SERVES 4

1 small mango, finely chopped

1 small red onion, finely chopped

½ cucumber, finely chopped

25g fresh coriander, chopped

Juice of 1 lime, plus some zest and 1 lime, sliced, for garnish (optional)

560g skinless salmon fillets, cut into bite-sized pieces

1 tbsp olive oil

12 tortillas

1 red chilli (optional)

CAJUN-SPICE SEASONING

2 tsp smoked paprika

1 tsp cumin seeds

1 tsp coriander seeds

1 tsp dried thyme or oregano

1 tsp garlic granules

1 tsp black pepper

1 tsp salt

Pinch of turmeric – optional

1 Add the mango, onion and cucumber to a large bowl along with the coriander. Squeeze in the lime juice and add a little lime zest too, if you like. Mix everything together. Set aside until ready to serve.

2 Create the spice seasoning by pounding all the ingredients to a coarse powder using a pestle and mortar (or use a blender). Alternatively, use ground spices if you have them.

3 Toss the salmon in the spice mix until fully coated. Heat the oil in a frying pan over medium heat and fry the salmon for 2–3 minutes on each side, then set it aside until ready to serve. It should be opaque and flake easily – be careful not to overcook it as salmon continues to cook after you remove it from the heat.

4 Toast each tortilla for 1–2 minutes in a frying pan over medium heat until warm and the edges just start to brown.

5 Assemble the tacos by topping the warm tortillas with the chopped salsa and salmon. You can also add some thinly sliced red chilli for extra heat, if desired. Serve right away.

Make it vegetarian
Swap the salmon for 450g halloumi or tofu in step 3.

Tarragon Chicken with New Potatoes & Green Vegetables

Tarragon was a herb I discovered during medical school. I used to treat myself to a tarragon chicken sandwich from the deli around the corner from the hospital once a week, but it wasn't until much later that I started cooking with it. Tarragon, chicken and cream are a match made in heaven!

SERVES 4

600g new potatoes

500g chicken breast mini-fillets

1 tbsp olive oil, plus 1 tsp for the vegetables

1 red onion, thinly sliced

4 cloves garlic, chopped

25g tarragon leaves, roughly chopped

200g baby spinach leaves

200ml single cream

3 courgettes, sliced

200g green beans, topped and tailed

1 knob of butter

Salt and black pepper, to taste

1 Scrub the potatoes thoroughly, then boil them in a large pan of water until soft, 10–15 minutes depending on size.

2 While the potatoes are boiling, pan-fry the chicken mini-fillets in 1 tablespoon of oil over medium heat. Turn the chicken fillets to cook both sides until they start to brown and the middle is opaque when cut. Remove from the pan and set aside.

3 Add the onion to the pan and sauté over medium heat. Once the onions soften and start to brown, add the garlic and cook, stirring, for 1 minute.

4 Return the chicken to the pan, along with the tarragon leaves and baby spinach leaves. Season with ½ teaspoon each of salt and pepper and mix well.

5 Once the spinach wilts, add the cream, bring to a simmer and keep warm while you cook the vegetables.

6 Fry the courgettes and green beans in a pan over medium heat with 1 teaspoon of oil and some salt and pepper to taste for a few minutes.

7 Drain the potatoes and serve with a knob of butter alongside the chicken and vegetables.

Make it vegetarian

Swap the chicken for 500g whole washed mushrooms. Skip step 2, cook the onions and garlic in oil and add the mushrooms in step 3 allowing them to cook for a few minutes before step 4.

Sea Bass with Black Olives

I tried a similar version of this dish at a friend's house and since then it has been a regular in our home. You can switch out the sea bass for any firm white fish. Serve with rice or boiled potatoes and your choice of seasonal vegetables for a delicious easy midweek meal loaded with plant points.

SERVES 4

500g new potatoes

1 tbsp olive oil

1 small onion, chopped

6 cloves garlic, chopped

1 x 400g tin of chopped tomatoes

1 tsp mixed dried herbs

400g/4 sea bass fillets

250g pitted black olives (Kalamata olives are delicious here)

200g green beans, topped and tailed

200g broccoli, roughly chopped

Salt and black pepper, to taste

25g fresh parsley, roughly chopped, to serve

1 Thoroughly scrub the potatoes and boil them in a large pan of water until soft, 10–15 minutes depending on their size.

2 While the potatoes are cooking, heat the oil in a pan over medium heat and sauté the onion until it becomes translucent and lightly browned. Once the onion is ready, add the garlic and continue stirring for a minute over medium heat, being careful not to let the garlic brown.

3 Pour the tomatoes into the pan and use the tin to measure half a tin of water. Add the water and herbs and season with salt and pepper to taste. Mix well and bring up to a simmer.

4 Gently nestle the sea bass fillets into the sauce and scatter the olives over. Cover the pan and cook over medium heat for 5–10 minutes to cook the sea bass. Once cooked, the fish will turn opaque and easily flake.

5 While the fish is cooking, add the green beans and broccoli to a large frying pan with about 50ml of water. Cover and cook over medium heat for a few minutes, stirring halfway. Then remove from the heat and keep covered until ready to serve.

6 Remove the lid from the fish pan, allowing any excess water to evaporate and the sauce to thicken as desired. Sprinkle with the chopped parsley and serve right away with the potatoes and vegetables.

Make it vegan
Substitute the fish in step 4 for 2 x 400g tins of kidney beans, drained, cooking for only 5 minutes.

Creamy Fish Pie

I am always talking about incorporating more vegetables into your diet. What sets this fish pie apart from other recipes you might find is that it incorporates three different vegetables, and by pairing it with peas and/or a side salad you can enjoy a total of five different vegetables in one meal. Don't worry too much about being exact with the weight of the sweet potatoes, potatoes and carrots, you can always make the topping a little thicker – and no one wants half a sweet potato left over from a recipe!

SERVES 4

500g (total) sweet potato, carrots and potato, roughly chopped

4 tbsp plain flour

400ml milk

150g baby spinach leaves

25g fresh parsley, chopped

¾ tsp salt

1 tsp black pepper

400g smoked cod or any smoked firm white fish fillets, cut into bite-sized pieces

150g raw peeled king prawns

320g boiled peas and/or 200g salad leaves, to serve

1 Preheat the oven to 200°C, 180°C fan, gas mark 6.

2 Boil the sweet potato, carrots and potato in a large pot of boiling water.

3 Whilst they boil, make the white sauce: add the flour and milk to a large saucepan over medium heat. Whisk well to combine and keep whisking until the sauce thickens. This will take a few minutes. Add the spinach leaves and parsley and stir to let the spinach wilt, then cook the sauce for a few minutes to allow it to thicken up again. Next, remove from heat and set aside. Add ¼ teaspoon of the salt and ½ teaspoon of the pepper.

4 Drain the boiled vegetables and mash them until smooth using a potato masher. Stir in the remaining ½ teaspoon each of salt and pepper.

5 Place the cod and prawns in an ovenproof dish. Pour the white sauce over the seafood and give it a stir.

6 Spread the vegetable mash on top. You can use a tablespoon to evenly distribute it in dollops across the top, then use the back of the spoon to smooth it out. Use a fork to create a rough texture on the surface; this will help it brown. Bake in the oven for 30 minutes.

7 Remove from the oven and place the whole dish under a hot grill for 5–10 minutes to achieve a golden-brown finish. Serve with boiled peas, green beans or a side salad.

Make it vegetarian
Swap out the fish for 500g halloumi, chopped into bite-sized pieces and add in at step 5.

Salmon Teriyaki & Noodles

This recipe is a staple in our house, it's so simple, my older son regularly makes it on his own. It's a great way of incorporating oily fish such as salmon into your weekly meal plans.

SERVES 4

200g dry noodles (or 500g fresh)

200g mangetout, cut in half

200g baby corn, cut in half

200g asparagus spears, roughly chopped

1 tbsp rapeseed oil

560g/4 salmon fillets

TERIYAKI SAUCE

4 tbsp low-salt soy sauce

2 tbsp sesame oil

2cm piece of fresh ginger, grated or minced

2 tsp honey

Zest of 1 lemon, juice of ½ lemon

TO SERVE

2 tbsp sesame seeds

1 spring onion, sliced

1 Add all the Teriyaki Sauce ingredients to a bowl along with 4 tablespoons of water. Mix and set aside.

2 Cook the noodles according to the packet instructions, then drain and set them aside.

3 Place the vegetables in a large frying pan with about 50ml of water. Cover and cook over medium heat for a few minutes, stirring halfway. Remove from the heat and keep them covered until ready to serve.

4 Heat a pan over high heat. Once the pan is really hot, add the oil and pan-fry the salmon fillets, skin-side down, for about 4 minutes until it's crisp and brown. To prevent it sticking to the pan, don't be tempted to move it whilst it cooks. Flip and cook the other side for 3–4 minutes until it's cooked through. When cooked, it will be opaque and should easily flake when touched with a fork. If your fillet is thick, it may need a little longer. Remove from the pan and set aside.

5 Into the same pan, pour in the Teriyaki Sauce ingredients and cook to thicken. Once you reach a thick sticky consistency, add the salmon and stir gently, ensuring it's well coated in the sauce.

6 Serve immediately, sprinkled with sesame seeds and the sliced spring onions, alongside the cooked noodles and vegetables.

Make it vegetarian
Swap out the salmon in step 4 for 450g tofu cut into 4 'steaks' and pan fry for a couple of minutes on each side to brown.

Turkey-mince Kebabs & Vegetable Quinoa

Quinoa is gluten free and a great whole-grain alternative to rice. It's packed with fibre, vitamins and minerals such as iron, folate, magnesium and potassium, and is an excellent source of complete protein for vegetarians. I love that it can take up any flavours you add, which makes it easily adaptable in recipes. If you fancy a change, switch up the vegetables in this recipe, swap the quinoa for couscous or the turkey mince for lean lamb mince.

SERVES 4

KEBABS

500g turkey thigh mince

1 small red onion, chopped

4 cloves garlic, chopped

1 tsp turmeric

1 tsp ground cumin

2 tbsp lemon juice

1 egg

25g fresh coriander, chopped

½ tsp salt

VEGETABLE QUINOA

200g quinoa

150g mangetout, roughly chopped, or peas

150g sweetcorn (frozen or tinned)

150g edamame beans (frozen or fresh)

400ml boiling water

Seeds of 1 pomegranate

25g fresh coriander, chopped

2 tbsp lemon juice

¼ tsp salt

TO SERVE

1 lime, cut into wedges

1 Preheat the oven to 200°C, 180°C fan, gas mark 6 and line a baking tray with baking paper.

2 To make the Kebabs, add all the kebab ingredients to a large bowl and use your hands to thoroughly mix them all together. Form 8 long shapes, each about the length and thickness of a sausage, and place on the baking tray. Cook in the oven for 20–25 minutes, turning halfway, or air-fry for 15–20 minutes at 180°C.

3 While the Kebabs are cooking, rinse the quinoa thoroughly in a sieve under running water, drain and add it to a large glass bowl. Add the mangetout or peas, to the quinoa along with the sweetcorn and edamame beans.

4 Add the 400ml boiling water to the bowl, cover it with a heavy plate, and microwave on High for 10 minutes (900w microwave). Adjust the time if your microwave is a different wattage. Remove the bowl from the microwave, keep it covered, and allow it to stand for 5 minutes.

5 Add the pomegranate seeds and coriander to the cooked quinoa along with the lemon juice and salt. Mix well.

6 Serve the Vegetable Quinoa and Kebabs.

Make it vegetarian
Omit the Turkey-mince Kebabs and just serve the Vegetable Quinoa on its own or add grilled peach and 450g pan-fried halloumi for a more substantial salad.

Prawn & Kale Coconut Curry with Sweetcorn Rice

This curry is super-easy to make, and as the prawns only take a few minutes to cook it can be whipped up quickly in the same time that it takes the rice to boil. Perfect after a long day at work. If you're using frozen prawns, defrost them first before using. For a more cost-effective curry and more plant points, use half prawns along with a 400g tin of chickpeas or black beans.

SERVES 4

200g basmati rice

320g sweetcorn (frozen or tinned)

1 tbsp olive oil

6 cloves garlic, sliced

1 tsp cumin seeds

300g kale, sliced, tough stalks removed

1 x 200ml tin of coconut cream

500g raw peeled king prawns

1 tsp turmeric

¼ tsp salt

1 red chilli, sliced (optional)

Side salad, to serve

1 Rinse the rice in a sieve under running water or rinse in a bowl, draining at least three times. Place in a large pan and cover with at least 1.5 litres of boiling water. Boil for approximately 10 minutes, then drain, stir in the corn, and set it aside. If using frozen corn, add it during the last 3 minutes of cooking the rice.

2 While the rice is boiling, heat the oil in a pan over medium heat. Add the garlic and cumin seeds. Cook until the garlic softens and is just starting to turn golden.

3 Add the kale and coconut milk to the pan. Cover and let the kale wilt down for a few minutes.

4 Add the prawns, turmeric and salt. Simmer the prawns, uncovered, until they are fully cooked; they should turn opaque and pink.

5 Finally, sprinkle the chilli on top, if you like, then serve the curry with the sweetcorn rice. You could also have a side salad.

Make it vegetarian
Add 2 x 400g tins of black beans or chickpeas instead of the prawns., adding them in step 4 to heat through.

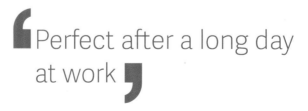

'Perfect after a long day at work '

Smoked Salmon, Dill & Lemon Pepper Spaghetti

If I gave my children this meal every day for the rest of their lives, I think they would be very happy! It is one of their favourite recipes and so simple to make that even my 11-year-old can whip it up. I serve this with a simple side salad, but a Rocket and Parmesan Salad would go well with this (see page 217). Use wholemeal spaghetti for more fibre.

SERVES 4

300g spaghetti

1 tbsp olive oil

4 cloves garlic, chopped

25g fresh dill, roughly chopped

200g smoked salmon

320g frozen peas

Finely grated zest and juice of 1 lemon

Freshly cracked black pepper, to taste

100ml single cream

Side salad, to serve

1 Cook the spaghetti in a pan of boiling water according to the packet instructions.

2 While the pasta cooks, add the oil to a large pan and sauté the garlic over medium heat for a few minutes until it becomes soft and starts to brown. Add the dill to the pan and stir for another minute.

3 Add the smoked salmon, frozen peas, about 100ml of the pasta cooking water and stir gently for a couple of minutes. The salmon will break into pieces as it cooks.

4 Season with the lemon zest (set aside a small amount for garnish), 2–3 tablespoons of the lemon juice and a grinding of black pepper. You won't need any salt as the salmon is already quite salty.

5 Drain the cooked spaghetti and stir into the pan. Finally, pour in the cream.

6 Garnish with more pepper and the reserved lemon zest. Serve immediately with a side salad.

Make it vegetarian
Add a 280g jar of roasted peppers, drained and chopped, in step 3 and omit the salmon.

Marmite Chicken

We used to live near a restaurant that made this incredible dish and it was always my children's favourite thing to order. So when we moved, I tried hard to recreate it at home for a 'Friday night in'. This recipe passed my children's strict standards, so I hope you enjoy it. Serve with rice and vegetables.

SERVES 4

250g basmati rice

600g skinless and boneless chicken thighs, cut into cubes

2 tbsp low-salt soy sauce

4 tbsp cornflour

4 tbsp olive oil

200g mangetout

200g Tenderstem broccoli

2 large courgettes, sliced

STICKY SAUCE

1 tbsp Marmite

6 cloves garlic, minced

3 tbsp honey

4 tbsp low-salt soy sauce

TO SERVE

1 spring onion, sliced

2 tbsp sesame seeds

1 red chilli, sliced

1 Rinse the rice in a sieve under running water or rinse in a bowl, draining at least three times. Place in a large pan and cover with at least 1.5 litres of boiling water. Boil for approximately 10 minutes, then drain and leave to stand for a further 5 minutes before fluffing up to serve.

2 While the rice cooks, add the chicken and soy sauce to a large bowl. Mix thoroughly, then sprinkle over the cornflour, and, using your hands, completely coat the chicken.

3 Heat the oil in a frying pan over medium heat. Fry the chicken until it is fully cooked and turns golden – the chicken will turn opaque with no pink bits. This will take a few minutes. Stir continuously for even cooking and a crispy coating. Set aside to drain on kitchen paper.

4 Add the vegetables to a frying pan with 50ml of water, cover, and cook for about 5 minutes until al dente. Set aside.

5 In a separate bowl, combine all the Sticky Sauce ingredients. Add the sauce to the vegetables in the frying pan and cook over high heat until the sauce thickens and starts to bubble. This will take a few minutes.

6 Add the cooked chicken into the sauce, ensuring it is fully coated, then remove from the heat. Garnish with the sliced spring onions, sesame seeds and sliced chilli. Serve with the cooked rice and some steamed vegetables.

Make it vegan
Break 450g firm tofu into bite-sized pieces to create a rough edge for all the sauce to stick to, and add to step 2 instead of the chicken. And use maple syrup instead of honey in step 5.

Mango Chutney Salmon

This recipe came to me one day when I was staring at a jar of mango chutney in the fridge that had been open for far too long and really needed to be used up, and I've never looked back. It is literally the quickest recipe ever to prepare and it tastes so good. Alternatively, use up any of those condiment jars lurking in the back of the fridge! I've paired it with Jeera Rice (see page 192) but it would be equally delicious with Edamame Quinoa (see page 161), a side salad or wrapped in naan.

1 Preheat the oven to 180°C, 160°C fan, gas mark 4.

2 Place the salmon fillets on a baking tray. Spoon 1 tablespoon of the mango chutney onto each fillet and spread it over to coat. Top with the lemon and onion slices and chilli, if using. Sprinkle the chopped coriander on top.

3 Bake in the oven for 12–15 minutes, or air-fry at 180°C for 8–10 minutes, until the salmon is opaque and flakes easily with a fork.

4 Sprinkle with the pomegranate seeds, if you like, and serve with the Jeera Rice.

Make it vegetarian
Swap the salmon for 500g paneer or halloumi, sliced into 4 'steaks'. The cooking time remains the same.

SERVES 4

560g/4 salmon fillets

4 tbsp mango chutney

1 lemon, thinly sliced

½ red onion, thinly sliced

1 red chilli, thinly sliced (optional)

20g fresh coriander, chopped

Seeds of ½ pomegranate (optional)

"It is literally the quickest recipe ever to prepare and it tastes so good"

One-pan Chicken & Spinach Pulao

When I don't have time to make a chicken biryani, I turn to my Chicken & Spinach Pulao, which can be whipped up in just 30 minutes. It combines elements of both biryani and pulao methods, resulting in a dish that may not be an authentic biryani but is a quick close second! Serve alongside a side salad of onions and tomatoes and with a dollop of yoghurt or raita (see page 102).

SERVES 4–6

300g basmati rice

1 red onion, chopped

1 cinnamon stick

3 black cardamom pods

2 green cardamom pods

1 tsp cumin seeds

1 tbsp rapeseed oil

4cm piece of fresh ginger, grated or minced

4 cloves garlic, chopped

1 tsp turmeric

1 tsp ground coriander

1 tsp salt

700g skinless and boneless chicken thighs, cut into cubes

1 x 400g tin of chopped tomatoes

200g baby spinach leaves

50g fresh coriander, chopped

50g fried onions (optional)

COOK'S TIP

For extra colour and flavour, add a few strands of saffron to 50ml boiling water, mix, and drizzle over the rice in step 7.

1 Rinse the rice in a sieve under running water or rinse in a bowl, draining at least three times. Place it in a large pan and cover with at least 1.5 litres of boiling water. Boil for 4–5 minutes to partially cook the rice. Drain and set it aside.

2 Meanwhile, fry the onion and whole spices in the oil in a large heavy pan over medium heat. As the onions start to brown, add the ginger and garlic. Stir for a minute, then add the turmeric, coriander and salt. Mix well.

4 Add the chopped chicken, cook, stirring, over medium-high heat and let it brown for a few minutes.

5 Pour in the tomatoes, bring the mixture to a simmer, and stir in the spinach leaves. Once the spinach has wilted, transfer half of the curry to a plate.

6 Layer half of the partially cooked rice on top of the chicken that remains in the pan, then place the rest of the chicken (the portion set aside earlier) onto the rice. Finally, add the remaining portion of rice on top. Sprinkle over the chopped coriander and fried onions, if using.

7 Cover with a tight-fitting lid and let it cook over medium heat for 5 minutes. Then, remove from the heat and leave the lid on for an additional 10 minutes to achieve perfectly fluffy rice.

Make it vegetarian

Use 500g paneer, chopped into bite-sized pieces, instead of the chicken in step 4.

Spiced Chicken Burger & 'Veg Chips'

'This is the best burger in the world,' said my son when I was testing this recipe, so I think it's definitely a keeper. It was so good my children asked me to make it again the next day! I serve it with vegetable 'chips' to maximise your intake of vegetables and colours.

SERVES 4

320g parsnips

320g sweet potato

320g carrots

60ml olive oil

4 skinless, boneless chicken thighs (about 600g)

100g panko breadcrumbs

1 tsp smoked paprika

60g black and/or white sesame seeds

½ tsp salt

50g plain flour

1 egg (or milk)

TO SERVE

4 burger buns

½ cucumber, sliced

1 large tomato, sliced

½ red onion, sliced

50g lettuce leaves

Mayonnaise or hot sauce

1 Preheat the oven to 200°C, 180°C fan, gas mark 6. Line a baking tray with baking paper.

2 Start by thoroughly scrubbing the vegetables and chopping them into long 'chips'. Place them on a tray, drizzle with half of the olive oil, and bake in the oven for 1 hour, stirring halfway.

3 While the veggies cook, prepare the chicken. Place the chicken between two pieces of baking paper and hit it with a rolling pin to flatten to an even thickness. Set aside.

4 Mix the panko, smoked paprika, sesame seeds and salt on a plate and set aside. Place the flour on another plate, then crack the egg onto a third plate and whisk it quickly with a fork.

5 Dip each chicken fillet into the flour to coat, then into the egg or milk, and finally into the panko mixture. Place the coated fillet on the lined tray. Repeat for each chicken fillet. Brush each fillet with olive oil on the top side only.

6 Place the chicken in the oven after the vegetables have been cooking for 30 minutes and cook for a further 30 minutes.

7 Once cooked, assemble the burger inside a bun with the cucumber, tomato and onion slices, and the lettuce. Serve with a squeeze of mayonnaise or hot sauce and the vegetable chips.

Make it vegan/vegetarian
Tofu works really well for the burgers instead of the chicken – coat it with flour and breadcrumbs as you would the chicken in step 5, but use non-dairy milk instead of egg for dipping. Use vegan mayonnaise if you like.

Hasselback Chicken & Sweetcorn Couscous

If you can Hasselback a potato, you can Hasselback anything, right? So, I decided to give it a go with a chicken breast. Easier than a Kiev and ready in no time, I paired it with a simple Sweetcorn Couscous for a delicious midweek meal. Adding sweetcorn or a tin of lentils or beans to couscous is an easy way to maximise your vegetable intake.

SERVES 4

1 tbsp olive oil

4 skinless, boneless chicken breasts (about 600g)

150g mozzarella, sliced

150g cherry tomatoes, cut in half

4 tbsp green pesto

50g baby spinach leaves

SWEETCORN COUSCOUS

200g couscous

200g sweetcorn (frozen or tinned)

2 tbsp pesto

150g baby spinach leaves

¼ tsp salt

½ tsp black pepper

400ml boiling water

1 Preheat the oven to 200°C, 180°C fan, gas mark 6.

2 Heat the oil in a frying pan over medium-high heat. Sear the chicken in the pan, on both sides for about a minute, or until they start to brown. Remove from the heat and place on a chopping board.

3 Make 4 cuts in each chicken breast, but not all the way through, creating small slits for stuffing. Stuff each slit with 1 slice of mozzarella, 2–3 tomato halves, ½ teaspoon of pesto and 1–2 spinach leaves.

4 Place the stuffed chicken breasts in an ovenproof dish and bake in the oven for 20–25 minutes until cooked through – the chicken will be opaque and no longer pink.

5 Whilst the chicken cooks, prepare the Sweetcorn Couscous. Combine all the couscous ingredients in a bowl. Mix well, cover the bowl with cling film or a plate and let it sit for 10 minutes. Remove the cover and fluff up the couscous grains with a fork before serving with the cooked chicken.

Make it vegetarian
Swap the chicken for a small aubergine or courgette. Skip step 2 and start at step 3. Bake for 30–40 minutes until cooked.

One-pan Sticky Orange Salmon

One-pan meals are always my favourite, everything in one pan means less washing up and an easy recipe, so it's a win-win situation! This is my Sticky Orange Salmon. A perfect recipe to incorporate your weekly portion of oily fish.

SERVES 4

560g/4 skinless salmon fillets

200g basmati rice

1 tbsp rapeseed oil

6 spring onions, plus 1 for garnish, sliced

2 tsp sesame seeds, plus more for garnish

400ml boiling water

200g broccoli, chopped

200g mangetout, cut in half

MARINADE

75ml low-salt soy sauce

3 cloves garlic, chopped

3cm piece of fresh ginger, grated or chopped

1 red chilli, sliced, plus more for garnish

3 tbsp honey

Juice of 2 oranges

1 To make the Marinade, combine all the ingredients in a large bowl.

2 Place the salmon fillets in the Marinade and refrigerate for 30 minutes or overnight, if possible.

3 When you're ready to start cooking, rinse the rice in a sieve under running water or rinse in a bowl, draining at least three times, then soak it in a bowl of cold water for approximately 20 minutes. Drain the rice just before cooking.

4 Heat the oil in a large, heavy pan. Add the sliced spring onions and sesame seeds, toasting them for about a minute. Add the drained rice and the boiling water. Stir the broccoli and mangetout into the rice mixture.

5 Arrange the salmon fillets, reserving the marinade liquid, on top of the rice and vegetables. Cover the pan and allow everything to steam cook over medium heat for 10–12 minutes, then remove from the heat and keep covered for a further 5–10 minutes.

6 In a separate frying pan, cook down the reserved marinade liquid over high heat for a few minutes. Stir continuously until the liquid transforms into a thick, sticky consistency. Drizzle some of the sticky marinade over the top of the cooked salmon

7 Finish by sprinkling with more sesame seeds, sliced spring onions and chilli before serving.

Make it vegetarian

450g tofu, sliced into similar-sized strips is a great substitute for the salmon in step 2. If you want to make this vegan, use maple syrup instead of honey in the Marinade.

Creamy Red Pesto Salmon

Salmon is a fish we include in our diet every week. Current advice suggests including at least one portion of oily fish in your diet weekly, as it is rich in heart-healthy omega-3 fats. For my family, salmon is a favourite, making this a regular meal in our household. Pair the salmon with rice or pasta. Add a side salad and broccoli for a complete meal.

SERVES 4

2 tbsp olive oil

560g/4 skinless salmon fillets

1 x 190g jar of red pesto

200g baby spinach leaves

½ tsp black pepper

100ml single cream

300g wholewheat pasta

320g Tenderstem broccoli

200g salad leaves, to serve

½ tsp chilli flakes, to serve (optional)

1 Heat the oil in a frying pan over high heat. Add the salmon fillets. Cook on one side for 4 minutes – to avoid sticking, do not be tempted to move them before the 4 minutes are up – then flip and cook the other side for 4 minutes. Remove the salmon from the pan, place it on a plate, and set it aside.

2 In the same pan over medium heat, add the pesto, spinach and pepper. Cook until the spinach wilts, then add the cream. Mix well and remove from the heat.

3 Cook the pasta in a pot of boiling water according to the packet instructions. Once the pasta is cooked, drain the pasta, reserving about 100ml of the cooking water.

4 Add the broccoli to a frying pan with 50ml of water. Cover and cook for about 5 minutes over medium heat until al dente. Set aside.

5 Add the 100ml of pasta water to the pesto sauce. Place the cooked salmon back into the sauce and warm everything together for a couple of minutes.

6 Drain the pasta and serve it with the salmon, broccoli and salad leaves. Add a sprinkle of chilli flakes to serve, if you like.

Make it vegetarian
Swap the salmon for 250g mushrooms and 1 x 400g tin of butter beans in step 1 and pan fry for a few minutes.

Miso Chicken, Rice Noodles & Vegetables

Miso paste entered my life around ten years ago, and I've never looked back. Although this recipe involves distinct steps for each component, don't be discouraged, as I assure you that each step is incredibly simple and only takes a few minutes. The result is a beautiful meal that effortlessly comes together in no time.

SERVES 4

3 cloves garlic, chopped

2 tbsp miso paste

2 tbsp low-salt soy sauce

3 tbsp rice vinegar or white vinegar

4 skinless, boneless chicken thighs (about 600g)

2 tsp olive oil

200g edamame beans

4 pak choi, cut in half

200g rice noodles

1 red chilli, sliced (optional)

CUCUMBER SALAD

1 cucumber

2 tbsp rice vinegar or white vinegar

1 tbsp low-salt soy sauce

1 tbsp black and/or white sesame seeds

1 Prepare the Cucumber Salad by thinly slicing the cucumber using a vegetable peeler. Place it in a bowl along with the remaining salad ingredients, mix thoroughly, and chill in the fridge.

2 Combine the garlic, miso paste, soy sauce, vinegar and chicken. Mix well.

3 Heat 1 teaspoon of oil in a frying pan over medium-high heat. Add the marinated chicken, with the marinade, and cook for 4–5 minutes on one side, then flip and cook for an additional 4 minutes on the other side. The chicken should turn opaque and easily break apart when cooked.

4 While the chicken cooks, place the edamame in a microwaveable bowl with a couple of tablespoons of water. Cover and cook in the microwave on High for 3–4 minutes, stirring halfway through. Alternatively, simmer them in a pan of boiling water for 6–7 minutes.

5 Heat the remaining 1 teaspoon of oil in a pan over high heat, then cook the pak choi for 2–3 minutes on each side.

6 Finally, place the noodles in a large bowl, cover with boiling water and let stand for 3 minutes. Drain and serve right away with the chicken, vegetables and Cucumber Salad. Add sliced red chilli, if you like.

Make it vegetarian
Instead of chicken, use 8 large Portobello mushrooms or slice 450g of tofu into 'steaks' and swap for the chicken in step 2. It will only need a couple of minutes each side to cook.

One-pan Lemon Pepper Chicken

This incredibly simple recipe makes for a perfect weeknight meal and is easy to prepare. I've opted for purple potatoes here. As we covered in Nutrition: The Basics (see page 15), purple foods are abundant in anthocyanins: powerful antioxidants responsible for their vivid colour and associated with various health benefits, including a reduction in inflammation linked to reductions in cancer and heart-disease risks. If purple potatoes are unavailable, white ones can be used.

SERVES 4

500g leeks, sliced

1 tbsp olive oil

6 cloves garlic, chopped

500g purple potatoes, thinly sliced (preferably using a mandoline)

2 low-salt chicken stock cubes dissolved in 1 pint of boiling water

500g chicken breast mini-fillets

1 lemon, thinly sliced

Black pepper, to taste

10g fresh parsley, chopped

250g frozen peas

2 corn on the cob, to serve

1 Add the leeks and oil to a heavy pan with a tight-fitting lid over medium heat and cook for a few minutes until softened.

2 Once the leeks have softened, add the garlic, stir for a minute, then layer the sliced potatoes evenly on top.

3 Pour the stock over the potatoes and vegetables, bring to a simmer, cover the pan, and cook for 10 minutes.

4 After 10 minutes, open the pan and add the chicken fillets with a lemon slice on each. Season with freshly cracked black pepper and a sprinkle of chopped parsley. Cover and cook over medium-low heat for 15 minutes.

5 Finally, uncover and add the peas to the pan. Cover and cook for an additional 5 minutes.

6 Meanwhile, cook the corn on the cob in a pan of boiling water.

7 To serve, cook off any excess water to reach the desired consistency and serve each portion with half a corn on the cob.

Make it vegetarian
Substitute the chicken with 500g sliced halloumi or tofu in step 4.

Smoky Paprika Prawns

This recipe takes me to the beautiful beaches of Spain. It is super quick to whip up and I serve it with a crusty baguette for dipping alongside a side salad. Alternatively, use half prawns and half butter beans for a more cost-effective dinner idea with more plant points.

SERVES 4

100ml olive oil

15 cloves garlic, sliced

2–3 red chillies, sliced

450g raw peeled king prawns

4 tsp smoked paprika

¼ tsp salt

TO SERVE

20g fresh parsley, chopped

Crusty bread

200g salad leaves

1 lime, cut into wedges (optional)

1 Heat the oil in a large frying pan over medium heat. Add the sliced garlic and cook until soft and lightly browned, being careful not to burn it.

2 As soon as the garlic has softened and starts to turn golden, add the chillies and prawns to the pan. Sprinkle in the paprika and add the salt. Stir everything together and cook until the prawns are fully cooked. They will turn pink and opaque once cooked through.

3 Garnish with the parsley and serve right away with crusty bread for dipping into the oil and some salad leaves.

Make it vegan

Swap out the prawns for 2 x 400g tins of butter beans in step 2.

'This recipe takes me to the beautiful beaches of Spain'

15-minute Meals

I call this group of recipes 'lifesavers', because some days I get back late from work and I need dinner on the table fast! Aside from the fact that I am not a nice person when hangry, I have two young children, so with these recipes I am able to respond to that 'what's for dinner, Mummy?' question in a flash.

So here are ten super-easy, super-quick recipes that you can turn to when you need dinner on the table ASAP. In fact, you can probably whip these up quicker than calling your local takeaway and placing an order. But whilst this is a quick dinner fix, you definitely won't be compromising on taste or flavour.

I love using the microwave when I can, because it allows me to toss all the ingredients into a bowl, let them cook, and not have to stand over a stove to watch over it. The recipes use mainly store-cupboard or freezer ingredients that you should have handy if you follow the advice in My Kitchen Staples (see page 41).

However, there's more to it than just the convenience factor. Preparing our own meals gives us control over the ingredients we use, allowing us to make balanced, wholesome dishes that provide the essential nutrients, vitamins and minerals that our bodies need to thrive.

Moreover, cooking at home is often more budget friendly and can easily accommodate dietary restrictions and preferences, whether that's addressing allergies, health goals or cultural inclinations. It ensures we nourish ourselves in ways that resonate with our unique needs.

Two-ingredient Pasta & 'Pesto'

I use the word 'pesto' in inverted commas here, as although this recipe creates a paste similar to pesto that is used with pasta in the same way, it isn't a pesto in the traditional sense. It's a recipe I came up with when I had a jar of sundried tomatoes in the fridge that needed to be used up, and I haven't looked back since. I've tried it with various jars of antipasti from artichokes to peppers and it works like a dream every time. I use cashew nuts as a more cost-effective alternative to pine nuts, and it also makes the sauce creamy without needing to add parmesan making it a brilliant vegan option. Try to buy jars of tomatoes in olive oil with garlic and spices and without any other additional preservatives or flavourings.

SERVES 4

250g whole wheat pasta

1 x 280g jar of sundried tomatoes in olive oil

100g cashew nuts

320g frozen or tinned sweetcorn

300g baby spinach leaves

1 tsp chilli flakes, to serve (optional)

1 Boil a large pan of water, add the pasta and cook according to the packet instructions.

2 While the pasta cooks, blend the whole jar of sundried tomatoes with about 3 tablespoons of the oil and the cashew nuts in a blender to a smooth paste/pesto. Adjust the consistency by adding a tablespoon or two of pasta water, if desired.

3 If using frozen, cook the sweetcorn by microwaving it in a covered microwaveable bowl for 4 minutes on High (850w microwave). Adjust the timings for different wattages. Or cook in a pan of boiling water for 3 minutes.

4 Once the pasta is cooked, drain it and combine in the pan with the spinach, 'pesto' and sweetcorn. Stir well over medium heat to wilt the spinach.

5 Serve with a side salad and a sprinkle of chilli flakes, if you like.

Microwave Butter Bean & Spinach Curry

If you're short of time, or it's the end of the week and you haven't had a chance to go shopping, this is a brilliant recipe that can be made with store-cupboard and freezer ingredients in just 10 minutes! If you've kitted out your kitchen as I suggested on page 41, then you should have all these ingredients handy to whip up this delicious meal. Serve with rice or naan for a nutritious balanced meal containing at least two of your five a day. This meal can also be made on the stovetop using the same method and timings.

SERVES 4

1 tsp cumin seeds

2 x 400g tins of butter beans, drained

300g frozen spinach

1 x 400ml tin of coconut milk

3 tbsp tomato purée

1 tsp turmeric

¼ tsp salt

Rice or naan

TO SERVE

a few coriander leaves (optional)

1 Toast the cumin seeds in a dry frying pan over medium heat for a minute to release the aromatics. Remove them as soon as they start to colour; be careful not to let them burn.

2 Combine all the ingredients, including the cumin, in a large microwaveable bowl and mix thoroughly. The bowl should be at least double the size of the ingredients to prevent overflow.

3 Cover with a heavy plate and microwave on High for 10 minutes (for a 850W microwave). Adjust the timing for different wattages.

4 Stir and serve immediately with rice or naan.

'If you're short of time, this is a brilliant recipe that can be made with store-cupboard and freezer ingredients in just 10 minutes!'

Fridge-raid Gnocchi

I call this Fridge-raid Gnocchi because it is exactly that: a gnocchi dish tossed together with anything and everything I can find in my fridge that needs to be used up – we are all about the zero-food-waste life in our house. I always keep a pack of gnocchi handy in my fridge or store cupboard for a rainy day when I need a speedy dinner. I've used baby corn, spinach and olives here, but any vegetables will work and if you don't have any fresh, use the trusted freezer supply – spinach, sweetcorn and peas all work really well and you maximise your plant points.

SERVES 4–5

150g pitted olives

320g spinach (fresh or frozen), roughly chopped

320g baby corn, cut into bite-sized pieces

500g gnocchi

1 x 190g jar of red pesto (or try my Two-ingredient 'Pesto' recipe on page 90)

Black pepper or chilli flakes, to serve

1 Place the prepared vegetables in a large pan with about 50ml of water. Cover and cook for a few minutes to retain their crunch, then set them aside.

2 Cook the gnocchi in a large pan of boiling water for 1–2 minutes until they rise to the surface of the water, then drain and add to the cooked vegetables.

3 Stir in the pesto to coat and serve immediately, topped with freshly cracked black pepper or chilli flakes.

'I always keep a a pack of gnocchi in my fridge or store cupboard for a rainy day when I need a speedy dinner'

Microwave Spinach Daal

Daal is my ultimate comfort food. I eat it by the bowlful, paired with rice, roti or even as a soup with a slice of hot buttered sourdough toast. It's so versatile and you can add in any vegetables you have handy. I've always made daal on the hob, but when I saw Shelina Permalloo, 2012 winner of MasterChef in the UK, make this daal in the microwave, I had to try it! You could use either method. Lentils are one of my favourite store-cupboard ingredients; they are cheap and incredibly nutritious. They are also a great source of B vitamins, iron, folate, protein and fibre.

SERVES 4

DAAL

1 tsp cumin seeds

300g dried red lentils

3 tomatoes, cut into small cubes

1 tsp turmeric

½ tsp salt

300g baby spinach leaves, fresh or frozen

25g fresh coriander, roughly chopped (optional)

TADKA

1 tbsp rapeseed oil

4 cloves garlic, thinly sliced

2 chillies, thinly sliced

1 Lightly toast the cumin seeds in a dry frying pan over medium heat until they become aromatic and begin to brown. Set them aside.

2 Add the lentils to a sieve and thoroughly wash them by rinsing them a few times under cold running water.

3 Place the cumin seeds, lentils and all the remaining daal ingredients plus 350ml water in a large microwaveable bowl that's at least double the size of the ingredients to prevent overflow in the microwave. Cover the bowl with a heavy plate to create a seal and microwave on High for 15 minutes (for an 850w microwave). Adjust the timing for different wattages. Alternatively, simmer on the hob in a large saucepan with a lid over medium heat.

4 While the daal cooks, prepare the Tadka. Heat the oil in a small pan over medium heat, add the garlic and chilli, and cook until softened and just starting to brown. Remove from the heat and pour over the cooked daal, then stir.

5 Sprinkle the coriander (if you have it) over the daal before serving.

Miso Noodle Soup

This miso noodle soup is incredibly easy to prepare in less than 15 minutes. You simply add whatever vegetables you have on hand, quickly boil the noodles in the broth, and serve. It's ideal for those moments when you need a speedy dinner option, and it's packed with plant points and nutrients. The recipe is also very adaptable; substitute tofu with leftover roast chicken, prawns or beans, depending on your preference.

SERVES 4

200g mangetout

200g red cabbage, thinly sliced

100g edamame beans (fresh or frozen)

3 spring onions, sliced

3 tbsp white miso paste

250g instant ramen noodles

2 tbsp low-salt soy sauce

200g baby spinach leaves

380g firm tofu, cut into bite-sized pieces

2 tbsp sesame seeds

1 red chilli, sliced, or chilli oil, to serve (optional)

1 In a large pan over medium heat, add 1.5 litres of water. Bring it to a boil and add the mangetout, cabbage, edamame beans, spring onions (reserving some for the garnish), and miso paste. Cook for 2 minutes.

2 Next, add the noodles, soy sauce, spinach leaves and tofu and cook for a couple of minutes until the noodles are cooked, or follow the instructions on the noodle packet.

3 Serve immediately, garnished with a sprinkle of sesame seeds, the reserved spring onions, chilli slices or chilli oil, if you like.

Easy Quesadillas

Discover the ultimate solution for those busy weeknights: speedy quesadillas filled with protein-rich kidney beans, fresh spinach and oozy melted cheese. These easy-to-make quesadillas can be whipped up in less than 15 minutes, making them the perfect go-to recipe when you need a delicious dinner on the table quickly. If you have courgettes or carrots handy, they can be grated and added in to maximise your plant points.

SERVES 4

2 x 400g tins of kidney beans, drained

8 tortilla wraps, or 16 mini wraps

200g baby spinach leaves

200g cheese, grated

SPICE MIX

1 tsp smoked paprika

1 tsp dried oregano

1 tsp garlic powder

1 tsp ground cumin

½ tsp salt

COOK'S TIP

Make extra spice mix and store it in an airtight container to save time on another day.

1 Create the Spice Mix by combining the paprika, oregano, garlic, cumin and salt in a bowl.

2 Place the kidney beans in a large bowl. Roughly mash or break them up using a hand blender or potato masher, then add the spice mix and stir well.

3 Place one tortilla in a frying pan over medium heat. Spread a layer of spiced kidney beans on it, followed by a handful of spinach leaves and finally the cheese. Top with another tortilla.

4 Toast for a few minutes until the tortilla starts to brown, then flip to cook the other side.

5 Slice into quarters and serve.

Microwave Chickpea Pulao

I know it may sound crazy, but you can create an incredibly fluffy and spicy pulao in just 15 minutes using the microwave. I must confess that when the idea first struck me and I began experimenting with the recipe, I had my doubts. However, I was delighted by how delicious it turned out to be. This dish has become a staple in our house, and it's so simple that even my children can prepare it. You can swap out the chickpeas for kidney beans or butter beans for variety.

SERVES 4

150g basmati rice

1 tsp cumin seeds

100g tomato purée

2 x 400g tins of chickpeas, drained

250g frozen spinach (no need to defrost)

½ tsp salt

1 tsp turmeric

2 green cardamom pods

1 tsp chilli powder

RAITA

250g Greek yoghurt

Pinch of salt

½ cucumber, grated

TO SERVE

30g fresh coriander, chopped

50g fried onions (optional)

1 red onion, sliced

1 large tomato, sliced

COOK'S TIP

It's important to use a very large bowl for this recipe; the total mix should only fill half the bowl at the most, but this avoids it overflowing in the microwave.

1 Rinse the rice in a sieve under running water or rinse in a bowl, draining at least three times, then drain and add to a large microwaveable bowl (see tip).

2 Toast the cumin seeds for 1 minute in a dry frying pan over medium heat. Reserve a third for the Raita and add the rest to the bowl along with all the remaining pulao ingredients. Mix well.

3 Cover the bowl with a plate and microwave on High for 15 minutes (for an 850W microwave – adjust the timing for different wattages).

4 While the rice cooks, prepare the Raita by mixing the yoghurt with a pinch of salt, roughly crush the reserved cumin seeds using a pestle and mortar, and add them in along with the grated cucumber. Stir together. Store the Raita in the fridge until ready to serve.

5 Remove the bowl from the microwave and let it sit for 5 minutes. Uncover and fluff up the rice before serving.

6 Sprinkle half the coriander over the rice along with the crispy fried onions, if using, and the rest over the Raita and tomato and onion slices.

Wrap 'Pizzas'

If you are Italian, please forgive me, as these are by no means authentic pizzas, however, some days I need a quick meal and loading veggies and cheese onto a tortilla-wrap base gives me pizza vibes in under 15 minutes! I usually pile them high with different toppings using whatever I have handy – spinach, peppers, mushrooms, onions, jalapeño, anything goes. You can use frozen vegetables, too; if using spinach make sure to squeeze out any excess water to prevent your base becoming too soggy.

SERVES 8

8 seeded tortilla wraps

1 x 190g jar of red pesto

500g mozzarella or 250g Cheddar cheese, grated

Toppings of choice – spinach leaves, red onion slices, sweetcorn, sliced mushrooms, sliced jalapeños

1 Preheat the oven to 200°C, 180°C fan, gas mark 6.

2 Place each tortilla wrap on a wire rack or a pizza stone and spread a thin layer of red pesto, using about 1 heaped tablespoon pesto per wrap.

3 Add your desired pizza toppings, then top with your choice of cheese and bake in the oven for 8–10 minutes, until the cheese has melted and the edges of the wrap are crispy.

4 Slice and enjoy immediately!

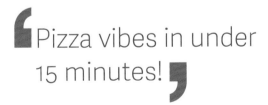

'Pizza vibes in under 15 minutes!'

Spiced Vegetable Frittata

Eggs are my go-to meal whenever I need something nutritious on the table fast. Eggs are a really good source of protein, iron, vitamins and minerals. Boiled, scrambled, poached are all great but my Spiced Vegetable Frittata is my absolute favourite. You can literally add any vegetables you have handy in the fridge – tomatoes, asparagus, peppers, courgettes, the list is endless – but for those days when you haven't been shopping, reach for the freezer stash, as I've done here.

SERVES 2

50g frozen peas

50g frozen spinach

50g frozen sweetcorn

4 eggs

1 tsp turmeric

1 green chilli, chopped or chilli flakes (optional)

½ red onion or 2 spring onions, chopped

1 tsp olive oil

50g mature Cheddar cheese (or your choice of cheese), grated

TO SERVE

Slice of sourdough and/or side salad

1 red chilli, chopped (optional)

2–3 chives, chopped (optional)

1 Place all the frozen vegetables in a microwaveable bowl and defrost them in the microwave for a few minutes or tip them into a colander under warm running water.

2 Crack the eggs into a large bowl and whisk with a fork.

3 Add the defrosted vegetables to the eggs, with the turmeric, chilli and onions. If you're using fresh vegetables, chop them as finely as possible, then add them to the bowl. Mix thoroughly.

4 Preheat the grill to its highest setting. Heat the oil in a large frying pan over medium heat. Pour the egg and vegetable mixture into the pan and cook for a few minutes until it begins to set.

5 Sprinkle the grated cheese evenly over the top, then place the pan under the grill and cook until the cheese starts to bubble and turn golden; this will only take a minute or two.

6 Enjoy right away, with a slice of toasted sourdough and a side salad.

Pick 'n' Mix Bowls

Making a 'Pick 'n' Mix' bowl is one of my children's favourite 'cooking' activities. The beauty of it is that there is hardly any cooking involved. It's more of a concept than an actual recipe. The more I think about it, growing up, most of my Indian meals revolved around this concept, albeit on a plate. It was usual to have daal, rice, two vegetable *shaks* (curries), salad and pickles all on the same plate. In this recipe, I've used store-cupboard staples to make my bowl, just to show you how easy it can be with limited ingredients. However, you can also switch it up and add fresh ingredients like cucumber, tomatoes and avocado. Smoked or fresh salmon would be delicious as a source of protein and oily fish. You can find some other ideas for different bowls in the images opposite, so get imaginative and maximise your five a day and your plant points in just one meal! P.S. The amounts are just approximate as a guide – jars and tins vary by brand.

SERVES 4

2 x 145g tins of tuna, drained

2 tbsp mayonnaise

2 x 400g tins of mixed beans, drained

2 x 400g tins of edamame beans, drained

1 x 300g tin of sweetcorn, drained

1 x 280g jar of artichokes, drained

1 x 340g jar of beetroot, drained

1 x 300g jar of pitted olives, drained

Black pepper, to taste

Chilli flakes, to taste

DRESSING

4 tbsp extra-virgin olive oil

2 tbsp lemon juice

1 tsp wholegrain mustard

1 Tip the tuna into a bowl with the black pepper and mayonnaise. Mix well and set aside.

2 Next, it's time to assemble the bowls. Split the beans, vegetables and olives between the 4 bowls and add some of the tuna mix to each bowl. Sprinkle with more pepper and the chilli flakes.

3 Make a simple dressing by mixing the dressing ingredients in a bowl, then drizzle over the vegetables.

Time-saving Traybakes

Traybakes are my go-to meals on busy days because they can be easily prepared, allowing the oven to handle the cooking while your hands are free to tackle the never-ending to-do list! In fact, I find traybakes to be the most time-efficient way of cooking for my family, despite the longer oven-cooking time. Quite often you can prepare a lot of the tray in advance, such as the vegetables, and store them in the fridge ready to pop into the oven the next day – perfect for days when I am working late. Using the oven for cooking may take a bit longer, but it's incredibly convenient not having to keep an eye on the stovetop all the time.

My top tip for success with traybakes is to ensure that all the ingredients have enough space to cook properly. So I always recommend using a very large tray for a family of 4 (at least 35 x 45cm) or, if you prefer, split the ingredients between two slightly smaller trays. If you have a large air fryer or are cooking smaller portions, the cooking directions for many of these traybakes, particularly the ones that don't use rice, can be adapted. However, you will need to adjust the cooking time according to your machine.

Thai Green Traybake

This has been the most popular recipe I have shared, and I've heard about countless remakes and had the most wonderful feedback, so I felt I had to include it in my book. For days when I need to be able to prep dinner fast it makes a super-easy option which lets the oven do all the hard work. You could mix it up by using any colourful seasonal vegetables to increase variety and plant points.

SERVES 4–5

200g basmati rice

1 lemongrass stalk

5 makrut lime leaves

5 spring onions, sliced

100g Thai green curry paste

400ml coconut milk

4 tbsp fish sauce

175ml boiling water

500g boneless, skinless chicken thighs, cubed

1 red pepper, cut into bite-sized pieces

100g baby corn, cut into bite-sized pieces

100g green beans, cut into bite-sized pieces

100g Tenderstem broccoli, cut into bite-sized pieces

1 tbsp olive oil

Handful of roughly chopped coriander leaves

1 red chilli, sliced (optional)

1 lime, cut into wedges

1 Preheat the oven to 200°C, 180°C fan, gas mark 6.

2 Rinse the rice in a sieve under running water or rinse in a bowl, draining at least three times, then drain.

3 Put the lemongrass, lime leaves, 4 of the spring onions, the Thai curry paste, coconut milk, fish sauce, boiling water and rinsed rice in a large ovenproof dish and mix well. Place the chicken so it sits on top of the mixture.

4 Cover the tray with foil and make sure to create a proper seal (this is crucial for the rice to cook properly in the steam; to be totally sure, use two layers of foil). Bake in the oven for 30 minutes.

5 After 30 minutes, remove the tray from the oven, transfer the chicken to a plate and stir the rice thoroughly. The edges might be more cooked than the centre, so ensure even mixing.

6 Stir in the chopped veggies, then place the chicken back on top of the rice and veggies. Brush the chicken skin with a little oil (this will help it to crisp up).

7 Bake, uncovered, for a further 25–30 minutes in the oven or until all the rice is cooked through.

8 Garnish with the remaining spring onion, roughly chopped coriander, sliced chilli and lime wedges. Serve right away.

Make it pescatarian/vegetarian/vegan
Swap the chicken for 4 fillets (about 560g) of salmon or 450g tofu, cubed, adding it in step 6 with the veggies. To make it vegan, swap the fish sauce for the same amount of low-salt soy sauce.

Peri-peri Traybake

Making your own peri-peri mix is incredibly easy – and believe me, it tastes far better than the pre-bought packets. If you've already gathered my top seven spices (see page 44), you'll have all the necessary ingredients to quickly whip it up for this traybake that's even more delicious than the one from the fast-food chain whose name starts with N! Serve this with a side salad of your choice and make it colourful – I love spinach leaves, tomatoes, cucumber and red cabbage drizzled with extra-virgin olive oil and lemon juice.

SERVES 4

800g potatoes, sliced into chips

2 tbsp olive oil

4 chicken thighs (about 500g)

4 corn on the cob

PERI-PERI RUB

1 tsp chilli powder

1 tsp garlic granules

1 tsp dried oregano

1 tsp ground cumin

1 tsp salt

TO SERVE

1 lime, cut into wedges

1 red chilli, sliced

1 Preheat the oven to 200°C, 180°C fan, gas mark 6.

2 Place the potatoes in a baking tray and drizzle with 3 tablespoons of the oil. Use your hands to mix and coat the chips with the oil. Bake in the oven for 30 minutes.

3 Prepare the Peri-peri Rub by combining all the ingredients and rub it all over the chicken.

4 Once the chips have partly baked, place the chicken on top. Brush the chicken with the remaining oil and bake for another 35–40 minutes, or until the chicken is cooked through – the juices will run clear when the chicken is pierced with the tip of a sharp knife and the meat will no longer be pink. Add the corn to the tray for the last 20 minutes of cooking. Top with the lime wedges and chilli before serving.

Make it vegetarian

Use 500g sliced halloumi instead of chicken in step 3, and add it to the tray for the last 20 minutes of cooking.

Spiced Salmon & Vegetable Traybake

This traybake is super easy and such a time saver on busy days. The spice marinade is really versatile, so you can use sliced halloumi or thin chicken fillets instead of salmon (just extend the cooking time for the latter by about 10 minutes). Asparagus is a great prebiotic, but it can be quite expensive out of season, so feel free to switch this up for a cheaper in-season vegetable. For optimal results, use a generously sized oven tray (around 35 x 40cm) for serving 4 people, or opt for 2 smaller trays to ensure even cooking of the ingredients.

SERVES 4

800g sweet potatoes, cut into 1–2cm cubes

1 tsp cumin seeds

2 tbsp olive oil

½ tsp salt

560g/4 salmon fillets

300g cherry tomatoes

350g asparagus, roughly sliced

320g red cabbage, roughly sliced

MARINADE

1 tsp Kashmiri chilli powder

1 tsp ground cumin

2cm piece of fresh ginger, grated or minced

3 cloves garlic, minced

2 tbsp lemon juice

1 Preheat the oven to 200°C, 180°C fan, gas mark 6.

2 Place the sweet potatoes in a large ovenproof tray; add the cumin seeds, oil and salt. Mix well and cook in the oven for 25 minutes.

3 While the sweet potatoes are cooking, prepare the Salmon Marinade by mixing all the ingredients together, then toss the salmon fillets in the Marinade to fully coat them.

4 After 25 minutes, remove the baking tray from the oven. Add the whole tomatoes, asparagus and cabbage, then nestle the salmon fillets in between the vegetables.

5 Return the tray to the oven and cook for an additional 12–15 minutes, or until the salmon is opaque and flakes easily with a fork. Serve immediately.

Make it vegetarian
Swap out the salmon for 500g sliced halloumi from step 3 onwards.

Harissa Chicken & Orzo Traybake

Using orzo in this recipe instead of rice makes the cooking process much quicker for a traybake. If you prefer your veggies with a slight crunch, skip step 3 and move from step 2 directly to step 4. I love the taste of rose harissa in this traybake, but if you can't find it, a jar of red pesto is an excellent alternative. Alternatively, you can try my two-ingredient sundried tomato pesto (see page 90). I often swap in chickpeas for half the chicken to increase my fibre and five-a-day intake.

SERVES 4

3 tbsp rose harissa paste (or 1 x 190g jar of red pesto)

500g chicken breast mini-fillets

200g green beans, sliced

3 different-coloured peppers, deseeded and cut into 1–2cm cubes

200g asparagus, sliced

½ tsp salt

1 tbsp olive oil

250g orzo

400ml passata

1 tsp smoked paprika

1 Preheat the oven to 200°C, 180°C fan, gas mark 6.

2 Massage the harissa paste into the chicken fillets and set them aside.

3 Place the vegetables in the baking tray, add the salt and oil, mix well, then bake in the oven for 15–20 minutes.

4 Remove the tray from the oven and add the orzo, passata, 150ml of water and paprika. Stir well. Nestle the harissa chicken fillets on top of the orzo. Bake in the oven for 20 minutes.

5 Remove from the oven and serve immediately.

Make it vegan
Substitute the chicken with 2 x 400g tins chickpeas in step 2 and use a vegan red pesto, if using pesto.

Citrus Sea Bass Traybake

The lemon, lime and orange add delightful citrus notes to this sea bass, which pairs so well with the ginger and soy sauce. Feel free to change the vegetables for seasonal options. For optimal results, use a generously sized oven tray (around 35 x 40cm) for serving 4 people, or opt for 2 smaller trays to ensure even cooking of the ingredients.

SERVES 4

4 pak choi, cut in half lengthways

5 tbsp low-salt soy sauce

1 tsp olive oil

380g/4 sea bass fillets

2cm piece of fresh ginger

1 lemon, sliced

1 lime, sliced

1 small orange, sliced

600g cooked egg noodles

300g asparagus or green beans, sliced

2 spring onions, sliced

1 red chilli, sliced

1 Preheat the oven to 200°C, 180°C fan, gas mark 6.

2 Place the pak choi in a baking tray along with 50ml of water and 1 tablespoon of the soy sauce. Brush with oil and bake for 10 minutes.

3 While it bakes, cut four large pieces of baking paper – they need to be large enough to fully enclose the fish fillets – and place a sea bass fillet on each.

4 Grate a little ginger and add 1 tablespoon of soy sauce to each fillet, then arrange the lemon, lime and orange slices on top of the sea bass fillets.

5 Fold and seal the baking paper – bring opposite sides together directly above the ingredients, then fold the edges over tightly in small, overlapping folds to create a secure seal. Finally, twist the ends of the package tightly to ensure a well-sealed enclosure. This method traps steam, which helps to infuse the flavours while baking.

6 Remove the tray from the oven, add the noodles and asparagus or green beans. Nestle the sea bass parcels in between and return to the oven. Bake for an additional 15 minutes.

7 Serve immediately, topped with sliced spring onions and red chilli.

Make it vegan

Use 450g sliced tofu instead of sea bass in step 3 and egg-free noodles for a tasty vegan alternative.

Hoisin Chicken Traybake

My children love hoisin sauce, so I wanted to come up with a recipe that would incorporate hoisin flavours into a traybake for a quick and easy meal. This way I can let the oven do the cooking, leaving me free to get on with my never-ending list of jobs! Another colourful vegetable-packed meal to maximise your five a day.

SERVES 4

4 chicken thighs (about 500g)

100ml hoisin sauce

200g basmati rice

4 spring onions, thinly sliced

200g edamame beans (fresh or frozen)

1 large red pepper, deseeded and chopped

200g green beans, topped and tailed

40ml low-salt soy sauce

25ml rice wine vinegar (or other white vinegar)

450ml boiling water

1 tbsp olive oil

TO SERVE

1 tbsp sesame seeds

1 chilli, sliced

1 lime, cut into wedges

1 Preheat the oven to 200°C, 180°C fan, gas mark 6.

2 Place your chicken in a large bowl. Pour the hoisin sauce over and use your fingers to thoroughly coat each piece. Set aside.

3 Rinse the rice in a sieve under running water or rinse in a bowl, draining at least three times, then drain and add to a large ovenproof tray along with the spring onions, edamame beans, pepper and green beans.

4 In a jug, combine the soy sauce, vinegar and boiling water. Pour this mixture over the rice and vegetables in the tray and mix everything well.

5 Nestle the chicken thighs into the rice and cover the tray with tin foil, ensuring a tight seal (this is crucial for the rice to cook properly in the steam, so use 2 layers of tin foil to be sure).

6 Place the tray in the oven. After 30 minutes, remove the foil and chicken and stir the rice thoroughly. The edges might be more cooked than the centre, so try to stir evenly.

7 Place the chicken back on top of the rice, brush with a little oil then return the uncovered tray to the oven for 30 minutes or until the rice has fully absorbed all the liquid and is cooked through.

8 Serve with a sprinkle of sesame seeds, sliced chilli and a squeeze of lime.

Make it vegan
Swap the chicken for 450g tofu, or smoked tofu, sliced into 'steaks' in step 2.

Pesto Chicken & Vegetable Traybake

This traybake is an effortless midweek idea that's both nutritious and delicious. Say goodbye to soggy broccoli, roasting it retains its crunch and enhances the flavour! For optimal results, use a generously sized oven tray (around 35 x 40 cm) for serving 4 people, or opt for 2 smaller trays to ensure even cooking of the ingredients.

SERVES 4

600g new potatoes, cut into 2cm cubes

1 tsp olive oil

½ tsp salt

1 x 190g jar of green pesto

500g chicken breast mini-fillets

1 red onion, sliced

350g broccoli, cut into florets

2 corn on the cob, halved

2 tbsp pine nuts

TO SERVE

a handful of basil leaves (optional)

1 Preheat the oven to 200°C, 180°C fan, gas mark 6.

2 Place the potatoes in a baking tray to form a flat layer, then drizzle over the oil and sprinkle with salt. Mix well to coat. Bake in the oven for 20 minutes until the potatoes are starting to soften.

3 In a large bowl, add 3 tablespoons of pesto to the chicken fillets and mix well.

4 Once the potatoes have baked for 20 minutes, add the prepared vegetables to the tray and nestle the chicken fillets in between them. Sprinkle over the pine nuts.

5 Bake for 20–25 minutes until the chicken is fully cooked – the juices will run clear when the chicken is pierced with the tip of a sharp knife and the meat will no longer be pink.

6 Drizzle the remaining pesto over the chicken and veggies, scatter over the basil leaves if using then serve immediately.

Make it vegetarian
500g sliced halloumi added in step 3 is a delicious alternative to the chicken here and make sure you use a vegetarian pesto.

'Say goodbye to soggy broccoli, roasting it retains its crunch and enhances the flavour!'

Mediterranean Cod Traybake

This meal has become a staple in our home, regularly gracing our midweek dinner table. For variety and sustainability, opt for coley fillets as a substitute for cod; not only is it a more environmentally conscious choice, it also offers a more cost-effective option.

SERVES 4

800g new potatoes, sliced into ½cm slices

1 tbsp olive oil

¼ tsp salt

320g green beans

200g cherry tomatoes

560g/4 cod or coley fillets

1 x 190g jar of green pesto

1 lime, sliced

200g whole pitted black olives (Kalamata work well)

2 tbsp pine nuts

½ tsp black pepper

TO SERVE

a handful of basil leaves (optional)

1 Preheat the oven to 200°C, 180°C fan, gas mark 6.

2 Place the potatoes in a large baking tray, add the oil and salt, and mix well to coat evenly.

Put the tray in the oven and bake for 30 minutes.

3 Take the tray out of the oven and add the green beans and whole tomatoes. Stir the vegetables to combine, then return the tray to the oven for an additional 20 minutes.

4 Remove the tray from the oven again and gently place the fish fillets on top of the vegetables. Spread a teaspoon of pesto over each fillet, then top with a slice of lime.

5 Sprinkle the olives and pine nuts over the fish and vegetables and put the tray back in the oven and bake for another 12 minutes.

6 Once done, drizzle the remaining pesto over the cooked traybake. Serve with a sprinkle of freshly cracked black pepper, and a few basil leaves, if liked.

Make it vegetarian

Use 500g sliced halloumi 'steaks' as an alternative to the fish in step 4, and make sure you use a vegetarian pesto.

Fajita Traybake

Fajitas are always a hit with my family, and making them in an easy traybake is a big hit with me. It means I can whip up a quick guacamole and a cup of tea while the vegetables are roasting! This is a brilliant recipe for increasing the variety of vegetables in your diet, and is packed with fibre. As an optional extra fibre and protein hit, or to make this meal stretch a little further, you can add a tin of black beans too. You could also swap the halloumi for 500g of thinly sliced chicken breast fillets.

SERVES 4

2 red onions, sliced into 1cm strips

3 coloured peppers, deseeded and sliced

500g halloumi sliced into 1cm strips

2 tbsp olive oil

Handful of fresh chives, chopped

200g soured cream

4–8 tortilla wraps

FAJITA MIX

1 tsp smoked paprika

1 tsp ground cumin

1 tsp ground coriander

1 tsp dried oregano

1 tsp garlic granules

½ tsp salt

GUACAMOLE

1 large ripe avocado

Juice of ½ lime

½ tomato, finely chopped

¼ red onion, finely chopped

25g fresh coriander, finely chopped

1 red chilli, finely chopped (optional)

1 Preheat the oven to 200°C, 180°C fan, gas mark 6.

2 Add the onions and peppers to a large ovenproof tray with the halloumi.

3 Prepare the Fajita Mix by combining the spices in a bowl. Sprinkle this mixture over the halloumi and vegetables in the tray, along with the oil. Mix well to ensure the veggies are coated in the spices and oil. Bake in the oven for 25–30 minutes or until the vegetables are soft and cooked.

4 Meanwhile, prepare the Guacamole. Peel and destone the avocado, then add it to a large bowl along with the lime juice, tomato, onion and coriander. Roughly mash the ingredients with a fork to combine. Add the chilli, if using.

5 Stir the chives into the soured cream.

6 Warm the wraps by toasting them in a hot pan for a few seconds on each side. Serve them filled with the vegetables, Guacamole and chive soured cream.

Black Bean Tofu Traybake

This traybake is ready in just 15 minutes! Yes, you heard that right. For days when you need something hands-free AND quick on the table, this recipe is the one. Keep a jar of black bean sauce in your cupboard for convenience and adjust the vegetables based on what you have to create a delicious and easy meal. You can also substitute the tofu with chicken thigh fillets; just slice them into strips and cook for 20–25 minutes. For optimal results, use a generously sized oven tray (around 35 x 40cm) for serving 4 people, or opt for 2 smaller trays to ensure even cooking of the ingredients. Mushrooms are a great source of vitamins D and B vitamins.

SERVES 4

200g baby corn, chopped into bite-sized pieces

200g pak choi/choy sum, chopped into bite-sized pieces

200g Tenderstem broccoli, chopped into bite-sized pieces

200g baby mushrooms (I've used baby oyster and chestnut)

450g firm tofu, cut into 4 'steaks'

4 tsp black bean sauce

50g whole cashew nuts

400g cooked egg noodles or udon noodles

1 Preheat the oven to 210°C, 190°C fan, gas mark 7.

2 Divide the vegetables equally between the two trays and add the tofu. Spread 1 teaspoon of black bean sauce over each tofu slice, ensuring even coverage. Pour 50ml of water into each tray, sprinkle over the whole cashews and bake in the oven for 10 minutes.

3 After 10 minutes, break up and gently place the cooked noodles in between the tofu and vegetables, then return the trays to the oven for an additional 5 minutes.

4 Serve immediately.

'For days when you need something hands-free and quick on the table'

Meat-free Monday

I grew up in a vegetarian household, so I was vegetarian for most of my childhood. To this day, the majority of our meals at home are vegetarian, which is why you may have noticed I always offer a vegetarian or vegan option with all my non-vegetarian recipes. People often have misconceptions about vegetarian meals, especially when it comes to protein intake, but hopefully this chapter will show you that it is possible to create balanced vegetarian meals with plenty of protein, as well as other macro- and micronutrients, right in your own kitchen.

Current research tells us that we should all be incorporating more plant-based foods into our diet, not just for the benefit of the planet but for our own health. A good place to start might be by introducing a 'meat-free Monday' into your meal plan, which over time could naturally evolve into more meat-free days each week. Many people find it challenging to completely eliminate meat, so a more flexitarian, predominantly plant-based approach to eating may be more sustainable in the long term. I always advise my patients that it's better to make small, sustainable changes for the long term than to make large, unsustainable changes that won't last.

At the same time, I think it is important to remember that not all vegetarian or plant-based foods are the same. When I talk about increasing the amount of vegetarian foods, I am not referring to meat 'alternatives', which can sometimes be highly processed and contain many additives.

Bean Burgers

These bean burgers are a nutritional powerhouse, packed with plant-based goodness. The inclusion of beetroot adds variety but also keeps them wonderfully moist on the inside, while the walnuts and sesame coating add a satisfying crunch. I typically serve them in a fully loaded brioche bun with carrot batons or a side salad. The burgers can be made the night before and stored in the fridge.

SERVES 4

150g cooked beetroot in water

80g walnuts, chopped

2 x 400g tins of kidney beans, drained

1 tsp smoked paprika

¼ tsp salt

1 tsp ground cumin

1 tsp garlic granules

50g panko breadcrumbs

4 tbsp white or black sesame seeds, or a mix of both

50ml olive oil, for frying

TO SERVE

4 brioche buns

Lettuce leaves

2 tomatoes, sliced

1 small red onion, sliced

¼ cucumber, sliced

4 tbsp mayonnaise

Sliced gherkins

200g carrots, cut into batons, or a side salad

COOK'S TIP

To make a beautiful 'pink mayo', mix the mayonnaise with 1 teaspoon of the liquid from the cooked beetroot packet.

1 Begin by draining the beetroot but reserve the water if you would like to add it to the mayo – see Tip. Grate the beetroot and squeeze out any excess liquid with your hands, then add to a large bowl with the chopped walnuts, kidney beans, paprika, salt, cumin and garlic granules. Use a potato masher to roughly mash the mixture and break up the beans so they are partly crushed.

2 Divide the mixture into 4 portions and shape each into a burger with your hands.

3 On a plate, combine the panko breadcrumbs and sesame seeds. Roll each burger in this mixture to coat them thoroughly. Cover and transfer to the fridge to chill, ideally for a couple of hours or overnight, as this helps them to hold their shape when frying.

4 When you are ready to cook the burgers, heat the oil in a pan over medium–high heat. Fry each burger patty for a few minutes on each side, cooking until they turn crispy.

5 Serve the burgers immediately, inside a bun, layering them with lettuce, sliced tomatoes, onions, cucumbers, mayonnaise and gherkins.

6 Serve accompanied by carrot batons or a side salad.

Thai Basil Tofu

This is a very easy midweek dish that I cook when I'm short on time. Thai basil is a staple in most supermarkets now, but if you can't get hold of it, just substitute it with normal basil. Better still, did you know you can soak the stalks of any shop-bought basil in water for a couple of weeks after removing the leaves for cooking? Once they root, plant them in compost and leave them on your kitchen windowsill for an endless supply of your own homegrown herbs. Serve this dish with Noodles, as I have here, or brown jasmine rice for a fibre-packed meal.

SERVES 4

1 tbsp olive oil

100g cashew nuts

4cm piece of fresh ginger, grated

350g broccoli, cut into bite-sized pieces

300g green beans, cut into bite-sized pieces

400g tofu or tofu puffs, cut into bite-sized cubes

25g Thai basil leaves

2 tbsp soy sauce

NOODLES

4 spring onions, sliced

1 tsp olive oil

500g cooked egg noodles (egg-free if vegan)

2 tbsp sesame seeds

1 Heat the oil over medium heat in a large pan or wok. Add the cashew nuts and toss for a minute or two until they start to brown. Then add the ginger, mix for a few seconds, and add the vegetables along with 50ml of water. Cover the pan and cook over medium heat for 6–8 minutes until the vegetables have started to cook; you want them to still have a slight bite.

2 Add the tofu, basil and soy sauce. Mix well, then cover and cook for a few more minutes.

3 To make the Noodles, toss the spring onions in a pan over medium heat with the oil, cooked noodles and sesame seeds for a few minutes. Serve right away.

Mushroom Tikka

This is a super-versatile recipe as the marinade can be used on mushrooms, paneer or even chicken (the cooking time will need to be increased to 40–45 minutes for chicken). It's delicious in the summer months on the barbecue, but can equally be cooked in the oven or air fryer. Serve it with a side salad, or for a more hearty meal it makes a delicious filling for naan. Just add chilli sauce or my Green Chutney (see page 193) and Quick Pink Pickled Onions (see page 199).

SERVES 4

1 tsp minced or grated garlic

1 tsp minced or grated ginger

3 tbsp Greek yoghurt

2 tbsp lemon juice

1 tsp cumin powder

1 tsp turmeric powder

1 tsp Kashmiri chilli powder

600g baby mushrooms, such as oyster or chestnut

4 naan and your favourite accompaniments, to serve

COOK'S TIP

If using wooden, rather than metal, skewers, soak them in water for 30 minutes before loading them up with the mushrooms.

1 Preheat the oven to 200°C, 180°C fan, gas mark 6.

2 Add the garlic, ginger, yoghurt, lemon juice, cumin, turmeric and chilli powder into a large bowl and mix well. Wash the mushrooms and add them to the mixture, making sure they are fully coated. Allow to marinate in the fridge for at least 30 minutes or overnight.

3 When you're ready to cook, thread the marinated mushrooms onto the skewers one by one (see tip). You should have between 8 and 12 skewers. Place these on a baking tray in the oven and cook for about 15 minutes or cook under a hot grill until cooked through and very slightly charred, turning halfway.

4 Serve immediately on naan with your favourite accompaniments.

'Delicious in the summer months on the barbecue'

Tofu & Vegetable Noodles

This is another fantastic zero-waste recipe that helps you utilise any leftover vegetables – feel free to switch out different vegetables based on what you have in your fridge. Having a block of firm tofu in my fridge is a staple, allowing me to quickly prepare this recipe in minutes at the end of a busy day. It's a complete meal on its own or pair it with my Salmon Teriyaki (see page 60).

SERVES 4

200g edamame beans, fresh or frozen

400g block firm tofu

2 tbsp olive or rapeseed oil

1 tsp ginger, minced/grated

200g Tenderstem broccoli, sliced

2 peppers – 1 red, 1 yellow, deseeded and sliced

200g mangetout

4 tbsp low-salt soy sauce

400g cooked egg noodles

TO SERVE

2 spring onions, sliced

2 tbsp sesame seeds

1 red chilli, sliced (optional)

1 To cook the edamame, place them in a microwaveable bowl with 2 tablespoons of water, cover, then microwave for 3–4 minutes, stirring halfway. Alternatively, cook them in a pan of boiling water for 7–8 minutes. Drain and set aside.

2 Pat dry the tofu with kitchen paper and cut it into 1–2cm squares. Heat the oil over medium-high heat in a large wok or frying pan, then lightly fry the tofu for a few minutes until it starts to turn golden. Keep tossing to ensure all sides cook evenly. Add the ginger and mix well.

3 Next, add all the prepared vegetables, soy sauce and 2 tablespoons of water. Cover and cook over medium heat for a few minutes until the vegetables start to cook but still have a little bite.

4 Finally, add the cooked noodles and thoroughly mix to warm everything through. Sprinkle with the spring onions, chilli (optional) and sesame seeds to serve.

Cajun Bean Enchiladas

When you need an easy midweek meal in a flash that the whole family will love and with extra bonus plant points, try these enchiladas. They are delicious, nutritious and so easy to make that even my kids can whip these up in no time at all. You can switch up the spinach for grated courgettes for a twist.

SERVES 4

2 x 400g tins of kidney beans, drained

4 seeded tortilla wraps

200g baby spinach leaves

400ml passata

150g mature Cheddar cheese, grated

CAJUN SPICE SEASONING

2 tsp smoked paprika

1 tsp cumin seeds

1 tsp coriander seeds

1 tsp dried thyme or oregano

1 tsp garlic granules

1 tsp black pepper

1 tsp salt

TO SERVE (OPTIONAL)

150g lettuce leaves, sliced

½ cucumber, sliced

1 red pepper, deseeded and sliced

150g cherry tomatoes, cut in half

1 carrot, cut into batons

1 Preheat the oven to 200°C, 180°C fan, gas mark 6.

2 Place the kidney beans in a bowl along with all the ingredients for the Cajun Spice Seasoning. You can use a hand blender to roughly blend the mixture, or you can roughly mash it with a handheld potato masher.

3 Take a tortilla and spoon a quarter of the kidney bean mixture onto it. Add a quarter of the baby spinach leaves, then wrap the tortilla around the filling. Place the filled tortilla into a large ovenproof tray. Repeat this step for the remaining 3 tortillas.

4 Pour the passata over the wrapped tortillas, sprinkle over the cheese and bake in the oven for about 30 minutes, or until the cheese is melted and bubbling.

5 Serve with a quick salad of lettuce, cucumber, red pepper and tomatoes – or any other salad ingredients that you like.

'Delicious, nutritious and so easy to make'

Spinach & Ricotta Lasagne

I love spinach and ricotta cannelloni or ravioli. However, when time doesn't allow for making either, give this Spinach & Ricotta Lasagne a go. Getting all the flavours with less preparation time is always a victory in my view. I must apologise, as I've included one additional spice beyond my usual 'top seven', and that is nutmeg. But if you don't have it, feel free to omit it; it will still be absolutely delicious. I always make a large portion of this and freeze half for a rainy day, but you can halve the quantity if you only want 4 portions. I like to serve this with a leafy salad and some slices of tomato and cucumber.

SERVES 8

4 tbsp plain flour

400ml milk

1kg frozen spinach, defrosted

250g ricotta

100g vegetarian parmesan, grated

½ tsp ground nutmeg (optional)

100g breadcrumbs

250g lasagne sheets

1 x 400g jar of passata

150g cheese, grated

1 tsp mixed dried herbs

Salt and black pepper, to taste

COOK'S TIP

You can swap half, or even all, the spinach for peas, if you prefer.

1 Preheat the oven to 200°C, 180°C fan, gas mark 6.

2 Begin by preparing an easy white sauce. Whisk together the flour and milk, then gradually bring the mixture to a boil while whisking constantly to thicken the sauce. Set it aside. While this is not a traditional béchamel, it's a simple and effective option.

3 In a bowl, combine the spinach, ricotta, parmesan, nutmeg, if using, breadcrumbs, ½ teaspoon of salt and a pinch of pepper. Mix well.

4 Now it's time to layer up your lasagne. In a large baking dish (approx. 35 x 25cm), place half the spinach mix and smooth it down flat with a spoon. Top this with a layer of lasagne sheets and repeat. Pour the passata evenly over the lasagne sheets, then add another layer of lasagne sheets. Finally, top the lasagne with a layer of the prepared white sauce, sprinkle the cheese on top and scatter the herbs over the cheese.

5 Bake the lasagne in the oven for 35–40 minutes, until the cheese has melted and is just starting to brown on top.

Paneer Hot Dogs

Hot dogs, but not as you know them! As we discussed earlier, hot dogs do come under the category of UPFs (see page 33), which means it is advisable not to eat them regularly. So here's an alternative that hits all the hot dog vibes. Serve with carrot and cucumber 'chips' for two of your five a day.

MAKES 8 HOT DOGS

400g paneer

4 tbsp Greek yoghurt

2 tbsp lemon juice

1 tsp chilli powder

1 tsp turmeric

1 tsp ground cumin

TO SERVE

8 hot dog rolls

Raw sliced red onions or Quick Pink Pickled Onions (see page 199)

Yellow mustard

4 carrots, cut into small, long 'chips'

1 cucumber, cut into small, long 'chips'

Green Chutney (see page 193)

1 lime, cut into wedges (optional)

1 Cut the paneer into long 'hot dog' sticks and soak them in boiling water for 10 minutes to soften.

2 Next, prepare the marinade by combining the yoghurt, lemon juice, chilli powder, turmeric and ground cumin in a bowl. Mix well. Place the paneer sticks into the marinade and coat them thoroughly.

3 Arrange the coated paneer sticks on a lined baking tray (I use a silicone liner but you could grease the tray with a little oil if you prefer) and grill under a high heat for a few minutes until they start to brown. Flip them over and repeat on the other side.

4 Serve the paneer dogs inside the hot dog rolls with freshly sliced red onions and a drizzle of mustard, alongside carrot and cucumber chips. Alternatively, upgrade them with Green Chutney and Quick Pink Pickled Onions.

'Hot dogs, but not as you know them!'

Silken Tofu Green Pasta

This is one of my absolute favourite pasta sauces, and it's (unintentionally) totally vegan! The silken tofu, spinach and edamame combination offers great sources of protein and plant-based nutrition. Combine it with whole-wheat pasta for a perfectly balanced meal made in no time at all.

SERVES 4

320g edamame beans (fresh or frozen)

250g whole-wheat pasta

1 tbsp olive oil

1 red onion, sliced

½ tsp salt

4 cloves garlic, chopped

400g baby spinach leaves

300g silken tofu

TO SERVE

Black pepper

1 red chilli, sliced

1 To cook the edamame, place them in a microwaveable bowl with 2 tablespoons of water, cover and microwave for 3–4 minutes, stirring halfway. Alternatively, boil them in a pan of boiling water for 7–8 minutes. Set aside.

2 Place the pasta in a pan of boiling water and cook according to the packet instructions.

3 While the pasta is cooking, heat the oil in a pan over medium heat. Add the onion and salt and pan-fry until soft and just starting to brown. Then add the garlic and fry for a couple of minutes until it starts to brown. Next, add the spinach and allow it to wilt.

4 Transfer this mixture to a blender and add the tofu. Blend for 1 minute to get a smooth green sauce. Pour this sauce back into the pan.

5 Reserve a little pasta water to adjust the consistency as required, then drain the cooked pasta and add it to the sauce with the cooked edamame.

6 Serve right away with freshly cracked black pepper and sliced red chilli.

Spiced Roast Vegetables in Naan

This is the recipe I turn to when I have lots of random vegetables in the fridge that I need to use up. Roasting tired-looking vegetables in olive oil and spices totally transforms them into the most delicious meal! Personally, I'm happy to eat them on their own with a drizzle of my favourite Green Chutney, but my family prefer them wrapped inside fluffy naan. This is also a great meal-prep recipe. I'll often roast a couple of these trays on a Sunday (or any time I'm turning the oven on and there is a spare shelf) and use the vegetables as a side dish during the week.

SERVES 4–6

400g paneer or tofu, sliced into thin strips

3 sweet potatoes, cut into small chips

1 cauliflower, chopped

2 red onions, sliced

1 courgette, sliced

1 pepper, deseeded and sliced

½ tsp salt

1 tsp cumin seeds

1–2 tsp turmeric

2–3 tbsp olive oil

TO SERVE

Green Chutney (See page 193)

4 naan or wraps

a handful of coriander leaves (optional)

1 Preheat the oven to 200°C, 180°C fan, gas mark 6.

2 Begin by soaking the paneer or tofu strips in a heatproof bowl of boiling water. This helps to soften it.

3 Place all the prepared vegetables into a large baking tray (or split them into 2 trays). Drain the soaked paneer or tofu and add to the tray as well.

4 Sprinkle over the salt, cumin, turmeric and oil, and massage these seasonings into all the vegetables.

5 Place the tray in the oven and bake for 30–35 minutes, remembering to stir halfway through. If you've cut the vegetables larger, the cooking time may need to be slightly longer.

6 Garnish with a few leaves of coriander, if using, and serve immediately with a drizzle of Green Chutney or wrap the roasted vegetables in a naan or wrap.

Paneer, Pepper & Pea Pulao

I like to call this the 'triple P' Pulao, although if you want to switch out the vegetables for alternatives you are welcome to use vegetables that don't start with P! You could also make this with brown rice; you will just need to add more water (500ml) and cook for longer (30 minutes). Fibre, variety, plant points – this recipe ticks all the boxes.

SERVES 4–6

200g paneer, cut into bite-sized cubes

200g basmati rice

1 tbsp olive oil

3 cardamom pods

1 tsp cumin seeds

1 tsp ground coriander

2 red onions, sliced

Pinch of salt

250g frozen peas

2 peppers – 1 red, 1 yellow – deseeded and cut into cubes

400ml boiling water

25g fresh coriander, chopped, to serve

1 Soak the paneer in a heatproof bowl of boiling water. Rinse the rice in a sieve under running water or rinse in a bowl, draining at least three times. Set both aside.

2 Heat the oil over medium heat in a large, heavy pan. Add the cardamom pods, cumin seeds and ground coriander, and sauté for a minute to temper the spices before adding the sliced onions.

3 Cook the onions with a pinch of salt until they start to turn brown and caramelise (the salt helps them cook quicker). At this point, drain the paneer and add it to the pan. Keep stirring and fry until the paneer starts to brown slightly; this will take a few minutes.

4 Add the drained rice to the pan, stir well for a few minutes to toast the rice and coat it in the oil. Next add the peas (no need to defrost) and the chopped peppers to the pan. Mix everything well.

5 Finally, add the boiling water, bring the mixture to a simmer, and cover it with a well-fitting lid. It's important to have a good seal to allow the rice to cook in its own steam.

6 Cook for 8–10 minutes. Remove it from the heat, but keep it tightly covered for a further 10–15 minutes to allow the rice to continue cooking and fluff up.

7 Remove the lid from the rice and mix slightly to reveal your perfectly cooked fluffy rice. Sprinkle with the chopped coriander and serve.

Cauliflower Cheese Dauphinoise

This is the story of when two of my favourite dishes, cauliflower cheese and potato dauphinoise, met, fell in love and lived together happily ever after. I am not sure I can make one without the other now. This is a decadent dish, but life is all about balance and when paired with a salad it makes a delicious balanced meal with lots of colours and plant points.

SERVES 6–8

5 tbsp plain flour

500ml milk

1 small cauliflower, florets and stalks cut into 3–4cm pieces

1 small broccoli, florets and stalks cut into 3–4cm pieces

½ tsp salt

1 tsp black pepper, plus extra to serve

2 Maris Piper (or similar) potatoes, very thinly sliced (use a mandoline if possible)

3 cloves garlic, finely chopped or minced

200ml double cream

150g mature Cheddar cheese, grated

125g mozzarella ball, torn into pieces

Salad of choice, to serve

1 Preheat the oven to 200°C, 180°C fan, gas mark 6.

2 In a large ovenproof pan over medium heat, whisk the flour into the milk to incorporate.

Slowly bring the mixture to a boil, stirring continuously. It will gradually thicken as you mix.

3 Once the white sauce has thickened, remove the pan from the heat and add the cauliflower, broccoli, salt and pepper. Mix well and press down to form a flattish layer in the pan. Layer the sliced potatoes on top evenly.

4 Stir the garlic into the double cream. Pour this mixture over the potatoes. Spread both cheeses evenly over the potatoes, crack some black pepper on top and bake in the oven for 45–55 minutes, until the cauliflower and potatoes are soft and cooked.

5 Enjoy with a large side salad.

'This is the story of two of my favourite dishes meeting and falling in love '

Lentil Bolognese

Try this lentil version and you won't miss your regular Bolognese. Pair it with spaghetti, use it to top a jacket potato or in a cottage pie — the possibilities are endless. Adding spinach and peppers to this means that, along with the onions and tomatoes, you can earn lots of extra plant points, as well as boost your vitamin C intake to help the absorption of iron.

SERVES 4

1 red onion, chopped

1 tbsp olive oil

Pinch of salt

250g dried red lentils

1 large red pepper, deseeded and finely chopped

4 cloves garlic, finely chopped

1 x 400g tin of chopped tomatoes

1 tsp mixed dried herbs

200ml boiling water

250g whole wheat spaghetti

200g baby spinach leaves

1 Place the onion in a pan with the oil over medium heat. Add a pinch of salt. Cook for a few minutes until the onions start to brown.

2 While the onions are cooking, thoroughly rinse and wash the lentils. Drain them and set them aside.

3 Add the chopped pepper and garlic to the onions and stir for a couple of minutes.

4 Next, add the lentils, tomatoes, mixed herbs and the boiling water. Bring the mixture to a simmer, cover the pan, and let it cook over medium heat for 15 minutes.

5 Meanwhile, cook the spaghetti in a pan of boiling water according to the packet instructions.

6 Once the lentils are cooked, add the spinach to the pan and stir until wilted. Add a little pasta cooking water if needed to adjust the consistency. Serve with the cooked spaghetti.

Kale, Spinach & Halloumi Curry

This is a slight twist on your typical palak paneer recipe. I always incorporate kale into my version, which not only gives the dish a vibrant green colour but also introduces extra veggies. One day, we ran out of paneer and used halloumi instead, and it turned out to be delicious. Now, we alternate between the two. Tofu would also be a great option, making this dish vegan. I served it with brown rice for a fibre boost but it would be equally as delicious with naan or rotli.

SERVES 4

200g brown basmati rice

400ml boiling water

1 red onion, roughly chopped

2 tbsp olive oil

Pinch of salt

1 tsp cumin seeds

5 garlic cloves, chopped

4cm piece of fresh ginger, grated or finely chopped

1–2 green chillies, chopped

1 tsp turmeric

1 tsp ground coriander

300g baby spinach leaves

200g kale, roughly chopped

50g cashew nuts

500g halloumi (or tofu) cut into 3–4cm pieces

1 Rinse the rice in a sieve under running water or rinse in a bowl, draining at least three times, then drain. Place it in a large pan along with the boiling water. Simmer over low heat for 30 minutes, then remove from the heat, cover, and let it sit for 10 minutes.

2 While the rice is cooking, add the onion and oil to a large heavy pan over medium heat with a pinch of salt until it becomes translucent and starts to brown. Then add the cumin seeds, garlic, ginger, chillies, turmeric and ground coriander. Mix well for 1 minute.

3 Next add the spinach leaves, kale and whole cashew nuts to the pan along with 500ml of water. Cover and cook for 5 minutes until they wilt.

4 Once the vegetables have softened, use a hand blender, directly in the pan, to blend the mixture until smooth. Let it simmer for a few minutes over a low heat, adjusting the consistency with a little water as needed.

5 While the sauce simmers. Fry the halloumi, tofu or paneer pieces over high heat for a couple of minutes in a frying pan with the remaining olive oil. Flip them to fry the other side until golden.

6 Stir the fried halloumi, tofu or paneer pieces into the curry sauce, serve with the brown rice and enjoy!

Mushroom Stroganoff & Edamame Quinoa

My kids are not fans of mushrooms, so I share this recipe with a caveat; I substitute half the mushrooms with a tin of butter beans so the whole family is happy. I used chestnut mushrooms here, but you can use any mushrooms you like – oyster and shiitake are delicious too. The edamame quinoa is a brilliant whole-grain, high-protein alternative to rice.

SERVES 4

200g dried quinoa

400ml boiling water

1 red onion, chopped

1 tbsp olive oil

4 cloves garlic, chopped

500g chestnut mushrooms

150g crème fraîche

200g edamame beans, fresh or frozen

Salt and black pepper, to taste

25g fresh parsley, chopped, to garnish

1 Start by placing the quinoa in a large microwaveable bowl with the boiling water. Cover and microwave on High for 10 minutes. Remove it and let it stand for 5 minutes. Uncover and fluff it up to serve.

2 While the quinoa cooks, add the onion to a pan with the oil and a pinch of salt over medium heat. Once the onion starts to brown, add the garlic and stir for a minute, being careful not to let it burn.

3 Next, add the mushrooms. Keep stirring over medium heat until they soften.

4 Finally, stir in the crème fraîche and add a little water to adjust the consistency to your desired level.

5 For the edamame beans, add them to a microwaveable bowl with 50ml of water. Cook them in the microwave on High for 4 minutes, stirring halfway. Alternatively, cook in a pan of boiling water for 6–7 minutes.

6 Stir the edamame beans into the cooked quinoa and serve with the mushrooms. Season with freshly cracked black pepper and garnish with the chopped parsley.

Miso Butter Bean Orzo

This is a speedy one-pan meal with all the umami from the miso paste. Feel free to swap out the butter beans for other beans and the vegetables for seasonal options. Red cabbage makes a great alternative vegetable and gives this dish a beautiful colour!

SERVES 4

1 red onion, chopped

1 tbsp olive oil

200g mushrooms (I used oyster), roughly sliced

250g asparagus, chopped into bite-sized pieces

200g broccoli, chopped into bite-sized pieces

1 x 400g tin of butter beans, drained

150g orzo

50g white miso paste

1 vegetable (or mushroom) low-salt stock cube dissolved in 500ml boiling water

200g baby spinach leaves

150g crème fraîche

Black pepper, to taste

1 Place the onion in a large pan with the oil over medium heat and sauté until it softens and begins to brown.

2 Add the mushrooms, asparagus and broccoli to the pan. Stir-fry for a minute before adding the butter beans, orzo, miso paste, stock and black pepper to taste. Bring the mixture to a simmer, then cover and cook over medium heat for 10 minutes.

3 Uncover and stir in the spinach leaves until they wilt.

4 Finally, add the crème fraîche and serve with freshly cracked black pepper.

'A speedy one-pan meal packed with umami'

Something Sweet

Welcome to my children's favourite chapter in my book – and not only because they are the chief developers of the Coconut Macaroon recipe on page 170! I am a firm believer in enjoying all foods in moderation, and I couldn't write a cookbook without adding a few of my favourite sweet recipes.

From no-bake desserts to easy banana breads, I've got you covered with my top ten sweet dishes that are guaranteed to impress your guests and that are, of course, super easy to make!

We have some healthier twists on regular favourites alongside more indulgent recipes, and for special occasions I certainly don't hold back.

While I love experimenting in the kitchen and swapping out ingredients from recipes to give them my own twist, baking is a science. So, my top tip is to carefully follow the recipe ingredients and steps to every measurement for the fluffiest cakes and crumbliest cookies. Where it's possible to swap out ingredients, I've suggested alternatives.

Happy Baking!

Lemon Drizzle Cake

Imagine a super-soft, crumbly cake drizzled in zesty lemon drizzle and you have the dream combination, in my opinion. I added rose petals because I like to be a little extra at times, but simple lemon zest or candied lemon peel for finishing touches will make this a beautiful showpiece for any afternoon tea.

SERVES 8–10

150g room-temperature butter

150g caster sugar

3 eggs, any size

150g self-raising flour

Zest and juice of 1 large lemon

80g caster sugar

Rose petals, to decorate (optional)

1 Preheat the oven to 200°C, 180°C fan, gas mark 6. Line a 900g loaf tin with baking paper.

2 Place the butter and sugar in a large bowl and mix well by hand or using a stand mixer.

3 Add 1 egg and 50g of the flour to the mix and beat together to get a smooth batter. Repeat twice more until all the egg and flour is incorporated. Stir in the lemon zest, reserving a little for decorating.

4 Pour the cake batter into the prepared tin and bake in the oven for 30–35 minutes until a skewer inserted into the centre comes out clean. Transfer to a wire rack and allow to cool slightly before transferring it to your serving plate ready to drizzle.

5 Make the lemon drizzle by mixing the lemon juice and caster sugar together to form a thick paste. If it is too thick to drizzle, add a little more lemon juice.

6 Poke some holes in the cake using a toothpick and pour the lemon drizzle mix all over the cake while it's still warm (the serving plate will catch any drizzle run off). Decorate with the lemon zest and rose petals, if you like.

'This is a beautiful showpiece for any afternoon tea'

Blueberry & Cinnamon Banana Bread

This trusty banana bread has been my favourite way of using ripe bananas for years. I use rolled oats instead of flour, and the bananas and blueberries are enough to sweeten the cake without adding any extra sugar. I often mix up this recipe by adding nuts (walnuts and pecans go really well) or dark chocolate.

SERVES 8

200g rolled oats, plus 1 tbsp extra for decoration

3 large super-ripe bananas

100g light olive oil or butter

3 eggs

100g blueberries, fresh or frozen

1 tsp ground cinnamon

1½ tsp baking powder

1 Preheat the oven to 190°C, 170°C fan, gas mark 5. Line a 900g loaf tin with baking paper.

2 Grind the oats in a blender or food processor until you have a coarse powder. Set aside.

3 Mash the bananas well until they form a pulp (I use a potato masher, but a fork works just as well!). Add the olive oil or butter and mix well, then crack in the eggs and beat well to form a smooth batter.

4 Toss the blueberries in the oat flour to coat, then stir the berries and flour into the batter with the cinnamon and baking powder.

5 Pour the mixture into the prepared loaf tin, sprinkle a few whole oats on top, and bake in the oven for 40–55 minutes (check every 5 minutes after 40 minutes) until the cake feels firm to the touch and a skewer inserted in the centre comes out clean.

Coconut Macaroons

These might as well be called 'lockdown macaroons', because during the COVID-19 pandemic, when fresh ingredients were hard to come by and lockdown restrictions limited supermarket trips and deliveries, these were our go-to bakes. They could always be whipped up with store-cupboard ingredients and kept my children busy in between home-school lessons, as they could easily make these entirely by themselves.

MAKES 16–18

1 x 397g tin of condensed milk
300g desiccated coconut
1 tsp vanilla extract
100g dark chocolate (optional)

1 Preheat the oven to 200°C, 180°C fan, gas mark 6. Line a large baking sheet (approx. 35 x 45cm) with baking paper.

2 In a large bowl, combine the condensed milk, desiccated coconut and vanilla extract, mixing together thoroughly.

3 Take about a tablespoon of the mixture at a time and mould it into a round shape using your hands or an ice cream scoop, then place on the baking tray. Repeat until you have used all the mixture.

4 Bake in the oven for 10–12 minutes until the macaroons just start to turn golden. Don't allow them to brown too much. Remove from the oven and transfer to a wire rack to cool.

5 They are now ready to eat, or if you like you can give them a coating of chocolate. Once the macaroons have cooled, melt the chocolate in a microwaveable bowl in the microwave by breaking it into pieces and heating on High for two to three 30-second bursts at a time until melted. Stir well after each heating.

6 Dip each macaroon into the melted chocolate and place it back on the baking paper to set. If you like, you can drizzle any remaining chocolate on top.

Coconut Quinoa Balls

Looking for nut-free snacks perfect for holidays or school trips? I've got you covered with these coconut and quinoa balls. With only five ingredients and four super-easy steps, they are nutritious, delicious and so easy to make – even my children can easily whip these up.

MAKES 15 BALLS

100g quinoa

200ml boiling water

1 tbsp cacao powder

50g desiccated coconut, plus 40g for rolling (optional)

2 tbsp chia seeds

3 tbsp honey

1 Place the quinoa in a heatproof bowl and add the boiling water. Cover with a plate and microwave on High for 10 minutes. Remove from the microwave, leave it covered and let it stand for 5 minutes.

2 Uncover the quinoa and add the cacao, coconut, chia seeds and honey. Mix thoroughly, allow to cool, then refrigerate for at least an hour, ideally two, until set.

3 Remove the mix from the fridge and take approximately 1 tablespoon of the mixture at a time, then squeeze it in the palm of your hand a couple of times to form a tight ball. Use your other hand to shape it into a rough sphere (see image below). Repeat until you have 15 balls.

If you like, you can place the extra coconut on a plate and roll each ball in the mix to coat.

4 Store the balls in the fridge in an airtight container until ready to eat. They will keep for a few days although they probably won't last that long!

No-bake Nutty Chocolate Squares

Only three ingredients, no baking involved and prepped in 10 minutes, have I convinced you yet? These little nutty squares of chocolatey goodness are basically made with ground almonds, peanut butter and chocolate. They are a perfect easy recipe for little ones to whip up – you should only need to be on hand for melting the chocolate, depending on how little they are!

SERVES 4

200g ground almonds

300g runny peanut butter

100g dark chocolate

10g flaked almonds and 10g rose petals, to decorate (optional)

1 Line a 900g loaf tin with baking paper.

2 In a bowl, combine the ground almonds and 200g of the peanut butter and pour this mixture into the loaf tin. Press the mixture down firmly with your fingers so you have a flat layer and place the tin in the fridge while you prepare the next layer. I often use the bottom of a small glass to flatten it.

3 Break the chocolate into pieces and place it in a microwaveable bowl. Microwave for 30 seconds on High, stir, then microwave in 10-second increments until it's completely melted.

4 Stir in the remaining 100g of peanut butter and mix thoroughly.

5 Remove the loaf tin from the fridge and pour the chocolate-peanut butter mixture on top. Flatten it with a spoon and sprinkle with flaked almonds and rose petals, if you like. Return the tin to the fridge and let it set for 1 hour.

6 Once it's set, remove it from the fridge, cut it into squares, and enjoy!

Make it vegan
Use vegan chocolate.

Oreo Cheesecake

This is the dessert you make when you have guests coming over. It's definitely decadent, but as I always say, life is about balance and food is there for enjoyment as well as nutrition. It's a super easy no-bake recipe that is guaranteed to please! My top tip here is not to over-whip the cream cheese and always do it by hand, as I find it just turns into a gloopy mess if I use the stand mixer for that part.

SERVES 10–12

450g Oreo cookies (3 packs), plus 60g mini Oreos to decorate (optional)

120g butter

500ml double cream

120g icing sugar

1kg full-fat cream cheese

1 Grease or line a 23cm cake tin, preferably a springform one for easy removal.

2 Start by making the base. Place the Oreos into a large silicone bag (no need to remove the filling) and crush the cookies by rolling over the bag with a rolling pin until they resemble coarse breadcrumbs. Remove about one-third of this crushed mixture and set it aside.

3 Melt the butter by placing it in a microwaveable bowl and heating on High in 10-second bursts until fully melted. Add the melted butter to the remaining two-thirds of the crushed Oreos and mix thoroughly. Press this mixture into the base of the cake tin to create a smooth layer. Place the tin in the fridge to set the base while you make the cream layer.

4 In a large bowl, whisk the double cream and icing sugar together until stiff peaks form. Gently fold in the cream cheese. Finally, fold in most of the crushed cookies that you set aside earlier (save a small portion for decorating).

5 Pour the cream and cookie mixture onto the cheesecake base and smooth it out. If you like, you can pipe some of the mixture on top. Return the cheesecake to the fridge and let it set for at least 4 hours.

6 Just before serving, decorate the cheesecake with the reserved crushed Oreos or with mini Oreos, if you prefer.

Choco-misu

Choco-misu is my children's version of tiramisu and it is their signature dessert for any dinner party. This is another super-indulgent dessert loved by my whole family. The added bonus of this recipe is that you will be left with a little hot chocolate to sip on whilst your dessert sets.

SERVES 8–10

2 tbsp cacao powder

300ml milk

500ml double cream

75g icing sugar

250g mascarpone

200g sponge fingers

1 First, make the hot chocolate by mixing 1 tablespoon of the cacao powder with a little milk in a large mug until you have a paste. Then slowly add the remaining milk, stirring continuously. Pop the mixture into the microwave for 1 minute. Set aside.

2 In a large bowl, whisk the double cream and icing sugar until stiff peaks form. Then add the mascarpone and slowly whisk to incorporate. Set aside.

3 Quickly dip one-third of the sponge fingers into the hot chocolate mixture and arrange them flat on a 23 x 23cm baking tray or tin to form a base layer. Be careful not to soak the fingers excessively, as they will continue to absorb moisture.

4 Layer one-third of the cream mixture over the sponge fingers. Repeat this process with the remaining sponge fingers and cream mixture until you have three layers in total. If you prefer, you can pipe the final layer of cream.

5 Finally, using a sieve, dust the remaining cacao powder over the top of the pudding.

6 Place the dessert in the fridge to set for a couple of hours until it's ready to serve.

Granola

There is nothing like waking up to the aroma of freshly baked granola on a Sunday morning. Personally, when it comes to breakfast, I am more on team savoury, so my favourite way of eating granola is actually as a dessert. I like to serve it with a dollop of Greek yoghurt and fresh berries, or in my 'granola split' (a banana sliced in half, served with thick Greek yoghurt and a sprinkle of granola, see left). I've shared cup and metric measurements here, as I tend to find it easier to throw all the ingredients in by the cup. You don't have to worry about being too exact with the measurements for this particular recipe, though.

SERVES 4

2 cups/200g rolled oats

½ cup/ 60g pumpkin seeds

½ cup/130g uncooked quinoa

½ cup/60g sunflower seeds

½ cup/50g walnuts

½ cup/60g pecan nuts

½ cup/ 50g cashew nuts

¼ cup/40g chia seeds

2 tsp ground cinnamon

3 tbsp /45ml honey

COOK'S TIP

Make extra and you can freeze the granola in an airtight container, with as little air as possible for up to 3 months. Defrost on the counter-top overnight.

1 Preheat the oven to 180°C, 160°C fan, gas mark 4. Line a large baking tray with baking paper.

2 Put all the ingredients except the honey into a large bowl and mix well. Add the honey and mix thoroughly to coat the other ingredients. Sometimes it's easier to do this by hand.

3 Spread the mixture out on the lined baking tray – you want a nice flat layer so it can bake evenly. Cook in the oven for 10 minutes.

4 Remove the tray from the oven, mix everything thoroughly, then return to the oven for a further 5–10 minutes until the granola just starts to brown.

5 Remove and leave to cool down completely (I leave it in the oven with the oven door open) before transferring to an airtight container and storing in a cool, dark place for 2–3 weeks

Mascarpone Truffles

Truffles are one of the easiest sweets to make, and they're a fun way to get kids into the kitchen (because who doesn't like chocolate?!). They're perfect if you are entertaining; you can literally prep the mix in minutes and just leave it in the fridge to set. Roll them in cacao powder, chopped nuts (pistachios work really well) or sprinkles.

MAKES ABOUT 20

300g dark chocolate

60ml milk

250g mascarpone

25g cacao powder

1 Break the chocolate into pieces and place it in a large microwaveable bowl, then microwave on High for 1 minute, remove and mix well. Continue mixing the warm chocolate, and it will continue to melt. Repeat this step again. After the second mix, the chocolate should have completely melted. If it hasn't, you can microwave it again in 10-second bursts. Be careful not to burn the chocolate.

2 Next, add the milk and mascarpone to the bowl and mix thoroughly to incorporate the chocolate. Put this mixture into the fridge for 2 hours to set.

3 After this time, place the cacao powder on a plate.

4 Remove the truffle mixture from the fridge and, taking 1 teaspoon of the mixture at a time, roll this into a ball in your hands. (Warning: this can get messy if your hands are warm!)

5 Roll each ball in the cacao powder and set aside on baking paper. Serve at room temperature or store in the fridge in an airtight container for a few days.

Almond & Hemp Heart Cookies

These cookies are one of my children's favourites. I love baking, so I sometimes try to make a few healthy switches in my bakes to incorporate more variety and nutrients. In this particular recipe I swapped out plain flour for wholemeal flour and ground almonds, and I added hemp hearts. Of course, I've added a little touch of spice, too, with the cardamom!

MAKES 14

1–2 cardamom pods

150g butter

100g sugar

1 egg

100g wholemeal flour

200g ground almonds

60g hemp hearts

1 Preheat the oven to 200°C, 180°C fan, gas mark 6. Line a baking tray with baking paper.

2 First, crush the cardamom pods using pestle and mortar. Remove and discard the husks, then grind the seeds to a powder.

3 Cream the butter and sugar together, then crack in the egg and mix well.

4 Add the flour, almonds, hemp hearts and ground cardamom, mixing thoroughly.

5 Take about 2 tablespoons of the mixture at a time in your hands and roughly roll it into a ball, then press it in between your palms into a rough round cookie shape. Place on the baking tray. Repeat with the rest of the mixture. The cookies will spread a little, so make sure to leave a couple of centimetres between each cookie on the tray.

6 Bake in the oven for 8–10 minutes until the edges just start to brown. Alternatively, bake in an air fryer at 180°C for 8–10 minutes.

7 Allow the cookies to cool and set before handling.

Friday-night Feasts!

Welcome to the final chapter of my book, undoubtedly my favourite one to write and shoot. Over the years, I've had the privilege of living and travelling around the world, and I have absolutely loved the opportunity to savour diverse cuisines and cultures. So in this chapter, we will embark on a culinary journey to visit some of my favourite countries. However, there are so many wonderful cuisines out there and not enough pages so I might just save the others for another book!

On a Friday night, I like to take the opportunity to explore my creativity, delve into new flavours, and indulge in more adventurous dishes, transforming our meals into magnificent feasts. It's become a tradition on my social media for me to share our Friday-night fakeaways every week, and my family love coming up with ideas for me to try.

However, you can rest assured that each recipe has been broken down and written to ensure that it is super easy to recreate. Every component is designed to complement the others, so whether you decide to make an entire feast or just elements from each recipe, I guarantee they will all be easy to recreate.

So get ready to embark on a gastronomic adventure that will elevate your Friday night dining and leave a lasting impression on your dinner guests.

187

Indian-inspired Feast

Butter Chicken

Jeera Rice

Microwave
Spinach Daal
(see page 97)

Spinach & Onion
Bhaji

Green Chutney

Kachumber

The first stop on our exciting culinary journey around the globe is India. The rich tapestry of Indian cuisine offers an incredible diversity that varies significantly from state to state, each boasting its own unique dishes and culinary heritage. It is impossible to encompass the entirety of India's culinary delights; so instead I've chosen a few of my favourite recipes to make a delicious family friendly feast.

My one recommendation is that you put the cutlery away and enjoy these dishes the traditional way by eating with your hands. Eating with your hands is something I grew up doing, and I have passed this on to my children. It's more than just a method of eating; it is a way of forming a deep connection with the food. Your meal will still taste incredible with cutlery, but it will be even better if you use your hands! Use your right hand only to pick up pieces of food, and tear roti or naan to scoop up sauce-based foods. You can also use your fingertips set against your thumb as utensils to pick up clumps of rice. Give it a try! For younger children, let the food cool a bit before diving in. Practice makes perfect, but it's well worth the effort.

'The rich tapestry of Indian cuisine offers an incredible diversity'

Butter Chicken

If you enjoy ordering butter chicken when you go to an Indian restaurant, you're in for a treat, because I've simplified this restaurant classic to just eight steps, making it easier than ever to remake. Additionally, this recipe freezes really well, so my top tip is to make a double batch and freeze some for a rainy day.

SERVES 4

500g chicken breast, cut into 3–4cm pieces

4 tbsp plain yoghurt

2 tsp ground turmeric

3 tsp Kashmiri chilli powder

½ tsp salt

75g cashew nuts

150ml boiling water

2 tbsp ghee or butter, plus a knob to serve

1 cinnamon stick

8 black cardamom pods

6 cloves garlic, minced

4cm piece of fresh ginger, minced

1 tsp ground cumin

1 tsp ground coriander

100g tomato purée

1 tbsp dried Kasoori methi leaves

1 tsp sugar

100ml double cream

handful of fresh coriander, chopped, to serve

1 Place the chicken in a large bowl and add the yoghurt, 1 tsp each of turmeric and chilli powder and the salt. Let the chicken marinate in the fridge for at least 1 hour, or overnight.

2 To cook, place the marinated chicken on a baking tray under a hot grill until it starts to char slightly, this will take a few minutes. Then flip it and repeat with the other side.

3 Soak the cashew nuts in a heatproof bowl with the boiling water and set aside.

4 Heat 1 tablespoon of the ghee or butter in a saucepan over medium heat. Add the cinnamon stick and cardamom pods for a minute to temper the spices and release their flavours. Stir in the garlic and ginger, and cook, being careful not to let the garlic burn.

5 Next, add the remaining turmeric, cumin, coriander and chilli powder. Stir well for 30 seconds, then add the tomato purée and about 250ml of water. Let it simmer for a few minutes over medium-low heat until the oil separates and comes to the surface.

6 Crush the methi leaves between your palms to release their flavour, then add them along with the sugar and the cooked chicken into the sauce.

7 Blend the soaked cashew nuts and their soaking liquid to a cream consistency. Add this to the curry and stir well.

8 Pour in the double cream and give it a good stir. Serve the dish garnished with a sprinkle of chopped coriander and a generous knob of butter.

Make it vegetarian

Swap the chicken for 300g paneer, cut into cubes, at step 1.

Jeera Rice

This is how I make perfect fluffy rice every time. It's totally foolproof and I find it much easier than measuring out water to boil it. I like to infuse the rice with the beautiful flavour of cumin, which perfectly complements any curry. I often add vegetables to my rice to increase our five a day intake, and my favourite way to do this is to add 200g of fresh or frozen peas or sweetcorn to the pan for the last 3 minutes of cooking, or stir in a tin of kidney beans.

SERVES 4–6

200g basmati rice

1 tsp cumin seeds

1 Rinse the rice in a sieve under running water or rinse in a bowl, draining at least three times until the water runs clear, to remove any excess starch.

2 In a large pan, combine the rice with at least 1.5 litres of boiling water and the cumin seeds. You should use enough water to ensure the rice is free to swim around and cook in the water. Simmer the rice for 10–12 minutes until it is almost fully cooked.

3 Remove the pan from the heat and drain the rice in a colander.

4 Allow it to stand for a few minutes, then fluff up the rice and serve.

Spinach & Onion Bhaji

Who doesn't love crispy, restaurant-style onion bhajis? It's hard to believe that you can make them at home in under 20 minutes. What I love most about this recipe is its adaptability; you can add various seasonal vegetables. Here I've added spinach, but during the Christmas festive period I often incorporate sliced Brussels sprouts, and in the summer I use thinly sliced courgettes or kale. You can air-fry these but they definitely won't be as crispy!

MAKES ABOUT 20

2 medium red onions, thinly sliced

100g baby spinach leaves, finely chopped

150g chickpea (gram) flour, plus 1–2 tbsp extra (optional)

½ tsp baking powder

1 tsp turmeric

1 tsp minced ginger

1 tsp minced garlic

50g fresh coriander, chopped

½ tsp salt

500ml oil

150–200ml water

Green Chutney (page 193), to serve

1 In a bowl, combine all the ingredients except for the oil and water. Gradually add half of the water and mix thoroughly. Slowly add the remaining water, about 10ml at a time, until you achieve a thick batter that coats the vegetables. Adjust the water as needed; if the veggies are quite wet, you may not need all of it.

2 If the batter is too loose and doesn't hold together, add one or two tablespoons of chickpea flour.

3 Heat the oil over medium-high heat in a large pan. Ensure it is not more than one-third full. To test if it's hot enough, drop a small amount of the mixture into the oil; if it starts to bubble and rise up, it's ready.

4 Drop heaped tablespoon-sized bhajis into the hot oil and deep-fry for a few minutes, turning frequently until they turn golden brown.

5 Remove the bhajis and drain them on kitchen paper. Serve them hot with Green Chutney.

Green Chutney

Green chutney is incredibly versatile, offering a burst of flavour that can enhance a wide range of dishes. Its fresh and zesty taste makes it an ideal dip for snacks like samosas and pakoras, while also adding a perfect accompaniment to grilled meats or sandwiches. Additionally, you can use it as a tangy dressing for salads, a vibrant spread for wraps, or even as a marinade for meats and vegetables. The possibilities are endless, and its ability to transform the simplest of dishes makes it a staple in any kitchen. My top tip is to always make double and pop half in the freezer for a rainy day. I picked up the genius tip to use an apple for sweetness and texture instead of sugar from my mother-in-law.

MAKES 200ML

50g fresh coriander

5 cashew nuts

½ small apple, peeled and cored

1 clove garlic, peeled

5 fresh mint leaves

1 tbsp lemon juice

1 green chilli (optional)

¼ tsp salt

1 In a blender, combine all the ingredients along with 2–3 tablespoons of water, until you achieve thick chutney resembling a smoothie-like consistency.

2 If desired, adjust the thickness by adding a little more water as needed.

Kachumber

I grew up eating this as a salad side with most meals, either that or thinly sliced red onion and tomatoes with cumin and salt. The perfect accompaniment to any Indian feast! Chop it small if you're being fancy; for weeknights my pieces get much larger!

SERVES 4

½ cucumber, diced

2 tomatoes, diced

1 small red onion, diced

Small handful of chopped fresh coriander

1 tsp chilli powder

Juice of ½ lemon

1 Place the cucumber, tomato, onion and coriander into a bowl.

2 Sprinkle in the chilli powder and lemon juice, and thoroughly combine all the ingredients.

3 Serve immediately.

Middle Eastern-inspired Feast

Baked Beetroot
Falafels

Homemade Pitta

Hummus

Quick Pink
Pickled Onions

Quinoa
Tabbouleh

The next stop on our whistlestop tour around the world is the Middle East. I love the fresh flavours of this region, and falafels are one of our family's favourites. I still remember the time I tried the smoothest hummus on a trip to Israel, and I've never turned back. Give my creamy, dreamy, perfectly smooth hummus a try, and you won't either! Plus, there's nothing quite like the aroma of freshly baked bread, and my easy mini Homemade Pittas are sure to become a regular in your recipe repertoire.

'I love the fresh flavours of this region, and falafels are one of our family's favourites'

Baked Beetroot Falafels

I love falafel but I can never be organised enough to soak chickpeas the night before – when I want falafel, I want them now! So my easy falafel recipe uses tinned chickpeas as a quicker alternative, which can then be baked rather than fried. This recipe makes enough to feed 4–6 with a few extra falafels left over, which I usually add to a salad for my lunchbox the next day.

MAKES ABOUT 24 FALAFEL

250g cooked beetroot

3 cloves garlic, chopped

1 small red onion, roughly chopped

50g fresh parsley, roughly chopped

50g sesame seeds

½ tsp salt

3 tbsp lemon juice

2 x 400g tins of chickpeas, drained

3 tsp cumin seeds

100g ground almonds

1 Preheat the oven to 200°C, 180°C fan, gas mark 6.

2 Grate the beetroot, squeeze out the excess water, and add it to a food processor along with the garlic, onion, parsley, sesame seeds, salt and lemon juice. Add the chickpeas.

3 Toast the cumin seeds in a dry frying pan over medium heat for a minute, or until they just start to turn golden, then add them to the rest of the ingredients.

4 Pulse the ingredients in the food processor until they are combined but not completely smooth. You want the falafel to have a slightly grainy texture, not be entirely smooth. Transfer the mixture back into the bowl and stir in the ground almonds.

5 The mixture should now easily hold its shape when rolled into a ball.

6 Take about a tablespoon of mix at a time and roll it between your hands into a ball and place on a lined baking tray. You should have about 24. Bake for 20 minutes. Serve warm.

Homemade Pitta

There's nothing quite like the aroma of freshly baked homemade bread. I must admit, I used to shy away from making my own pitta for years. BUT once you've prepared them fresh at home with this super-easy recipe, I guarantee you'll never go back to store-bought.

MAKES 12 MINI PITTA

250g strong white bread flour, plus extra for dusting

1 tsp instant yeast

½ tsp sugar

½ tsp salt

1 tbsp olive oil, plus 1 tsp extra for proving

160ml water, at room temperature

ZA'ATAR (OPTIONAL)

½ tsp cumin seeds

½ tsp coriander seeds

1 tsp sesame seeds

½ tsp sumac

¼ tsp salt

½ tsp dried thyme or oregano

1 To prepare the dough, combine the flour, yeast, sugar, salt and 1 tablespoon of olive oil in a bowl. Gradually add the water and mix until a dough forms. Knead the dough well for about 10 minutes, or use a stand mixer with a dough hook attachment.

2 Grease a large, clean bowl with 1 teaspoon of oil and add the dough. Cover the bowl with a damp cloth and let it rest for 2 hours to allow the dough to rise.

3 Preheat the oven to 260°C, 240°C fan, gas mark 9. Line a baking tray with baking parchment.

4 Sprinkle some flour on your countertop and divide the dough into 3 portions. Divide each of these portions into 4 equal-sized pieces, resulting in 12 portions in total. Take each piece of dough and roll it into a mini pitta shape, approximately ½cm thick.

5 Optional To make the za'atar seasoning, add the cumin, coriander and sesame seeds to a pan over medium heat. Toast them for about a minute, stirring constantly to prevent burning. Crush them roughly using a pestle and mortar and mix with the remaining za'atar ingredients. Sprinkle this mixture on top of the pittas just before baking.

6 Place the pittas on the baking tray and bake for 6–8 minutes or until the pittas start to turn golden and puff up.

Hummus

The secret to the creamiest, dreamiest hummus is to overcook your chickpeas in water with bicarbonate of soda. Why? Because the bicarbonate of soda turns the water alkaline, which helps to break down the skins and chickpeas. That way, when you come to blend, you'll achieve the smoothest consistency. Another top tip is to blend with a couple of ice cubes in the mix; this helps to trap air bubbles. Use both of these tips for the BEST hummus ever!

SERVES 4

1 x 400g tin of chickpeas, drained

½ tsp bicarbonate of soda

1–2 cloves garlic

3 tbsp tahini

3 tbsp extra-virgin olive oil, plus more for drizzling

3 tbsp lemon juice

¼ tsp salt

2 ice cubes

za'atar seasoning, optional (see left)

1 Place the chickpeas in a large pan of boiling water with the bicarbonate of soda. Boil for 5–8 minutes until they are very soft and crumble easily between your fingers.

2 Drain the chickpeas well and add them to a blender along with all the other ingredients. Blend the mixture until it reaches a smooth paste.

3 Drizzle with extra-virgin olive oil before serving.

Quick Pink Pickled Onions

I keep a jar of these pink pickled onions in the fridge handy for all sorts of uses, not just as part of my Middle Eastern-inspired feast. I use them on my Paneer Hot Dogs (see page 146), as a side to a curry, or in salads to add a kick. The possibilities are endless!

SERVES 4

150ml white vinegar

1 tsp sugar

2 bay leaves

½ tsp coriander seeds

½ tsp peppercorns

1 large red onion, thinly sliced into rounds

1 Heat all the ingredients, except the onion, plus 150ml water in a saucepan over medium heat until the sugar has dissolved. This will only take a minute or so. Leave the mixture to cool.

2 Add the onions to a clean or sterilised glass jar with an airtight lid (old jam jars work perfectly for this purpose!). Pour the cooled vinegar mixture over the onions, seal the jar, and keep it in the fridge until ready to use.

3 The onions will be ready to use after about 30 minutes, or you can store them in an airtight container in the fridge until you need them. Just make sure the vinegar covers the onions completely.

Quinoa Tabbouleh

Tabbouleh is traditionally made with bulgur wheat, so feel free to swap out the quinoa for bulgur if you like. Both versions are equally as delicious, so I like to mix it up. Quinoa and bulgur make great alternatives to rice in dishes, too, as they contain more fibre and protein than rice.

SERVES 4

75g quinoa

50g fresh flat-leaf parsley, finely chopped

5 spring onions, finely chopped

2 cloves garlic, finely chopped

About 15 fresh mint leaves, finely chopped (or 2 tsp dried mint)

150g tomatoes, finely chopped

½ tsp salt

½ tsp black pepper

4 tbsp lemon juice

4 tbsp olive oil

1 Cook the quinoa in a large pan of boiling water or 10 minutes. Drain and set it aside to cool down.

2 Add all the other ingredients to a large bowl.

3 Once the quinoa has cooled, add it to the bowl and mix everything well. Serve immediately.

Chinese-inspired Feast

Sesame Prawn Toast

Satay-style Chicken

Egg-fried Rice with Peas

Pak Choi, Garlic Green Beans & Mangetout

Bring the Chinese takeaway home with my simplified recipes to make this feast! The Sesame Prawn Toast is one of my children's favourites and I often make the Egg-fried Rice with Peas with extra vegetables and tofu as a standalone meal. Whether you choose to make individual recipes or the entire feast, I promise this is going to elevate your Friday night in!

'I promise this is going to elevate your Friday night in!'

Sesame Prawn Toast

I always order sesame prawn toast when I'm in a Chinese restaurant, but it was only a few years ago that I learned how easy it is to make at home myself. It's so simple, and by making it myself, I can adjust the seasoning, use a multi-seeded bread and also air-fry the toast to make a healthier version.

MAKES 4

½ red chilli, roughly chopped

2 spring onions, roughly chopped

4 cloves garlic, roughly chopped

2–3cm piece of fresh ginger, roughly chopped

150g raw deveined prawns

1 tbsp low-salt soy sauce

4 slices seeded brown bread

80g sesame seeds (I used half black and half white)

8 tbsp olive oil, for frying

4 tbsp sweet chilli sauce, to serve

1 Add the chilli, spring onions, garlic and ginger to a blender or small food processor along with the prawns) and soy sauce. Blend until you have a paste.

2 Spread this paste evenly over your 4 slices of bread.

3 Next, spread the sesame seeds out flat on a plate. Dip the prawn side of each slice of bread into the sesame seeds to coat the prawn mixture. Set aside.

4 Heat 2 tablespoons of oil at a time in a frying pan over medium heat. Fry each toast for about 2 minutes on each side until they turn golden and crispy. Alternatively, you can air-fry the bread – just brush it with a little oil and air-fry at 200°C for 10 minutes.

5 Serve with a sweet chilli sauce to dip.

Make it vegan

Substitute the prawns for the same quantity of firm tofu from step 1.

Satay-style Chicken

This is a simplified chicken satay-style dish that my family loves. It's super easy to cook up for a weekday meal or as part of this feast.

SERVES 4

1 tsp sesame oil

3–4 cloves garlic, finely chopped or minced

4cm piece of fresh ginger, grated

500g boneless, skinless chicken thighs, cut into cubes or strips

1 tbsp low-salt soy sauce

1 spring onion, thinly sliced

Handful of salted peanuts, roughly chopped

SAUCE

3 tbsp peanut butter

70ml coconut milk

2 tbsp low-salt soy sauce

1 To make the sauce, mix the peanut butter, coconut milk and soy sauce together in a pan over medium heat. Slowly stir for 2–3 minutes until you have a smooth sauce. You can add a splash of water to adjust the consistency if you wish. Set this aside.

2 Add the oil to a large frying pan or wok over medium heat. Add the garlic and ginger and stir for a minute until the garlic starts to turn golden. At this point, add the chicken and soy sauce. Continue cooking and stirring over medium heat until the chicken is fully cooked. It should be fully opaque all the way through, and you should be able to cut through it easily.

3 Pour the sauce you made earlier over the chicken and mix well. Sprinkle the spring onions and peanuts on top to serve.

Make it vegetarian

Substitute the chicken thighs for 450g firm tofu, cut into cubes or rehydrated soya pieces in step 2.

Egg-fried Rice with Peas

I've always added lots of peas to my egg-fried rice to increase the vegetable content. This recipe is sufficient for four people when served alongside the rest of this 'feast'. Occasionally, I will also add diced tofu, mangetout and baby corn to make it a complete meal in itself. If you are making this a standalone meal in this way, you will need to double the quantity.

SERVES 4

100g rice

100g fresh or frozen petit pois/garden peas

2 eggs

1 tbsp olive oil

2 spring onions, sliced

2 tbsp low-salt soy sauce

1 Rinse the rice in a sieve under running water or rinse in a bowl, draining at least three times. Drain and cook for 8–10 minutes (see page 192). You want it just slightly undercooked. Drain and set it aside.

2 If using frozen peas, defrost them by running them under water in a colander for a couple of minutes.

3 Crack the eggs into a bowl and whisk them with a fork.

4 Heat the oil in a large wok or pan over high heat, then pour in the eggs and reduce the heat to medium. Stir the eggs to break them up and cook them.

5 Next, add the cooked rice, peas and spring onions into the wok. Keep cooking and mixing over medium-high heat to prevent it sticking.

6 Finally, add the soy sauce, stir well, and serve right away.

Pak Choi, Garlic Green Beans & Mangetout

As always, vegetables play an equal part in all my meals. Feel free to mix up the vegetables based on what's in season. In the UK, I find that you can easily grow your own pak choi for a lot of the year, as it thrives in the colder climate and is so happy in pots – you can harvest it from seed in just 6 weeks, or even less for baby pak choi! So why not try growing your own?

SERVES 4

2 tsp olive oil

2 large (or 4 baby) pak choi, sliced in half

1 tbsp low-salt soy sauce

4 cloves garlic, thinly sliced

200g green beans, topped and tailed

200g mangetout

½ tsp salt

sesame seeds, to serve

1 Heat 1 teaspoon of oil in a frying pan over high heat. Add the sliced pak choi flat side down, then add the soy sauce and 50ml of water. Cover and cook for about 2 minutes until it starts to brown. Flip and do the same for the other side.

2 Heat the remaining 1 teaspoon of oil in a frying pan over medium heat and add the garlic. Fry until it starts to turn golden, then add the green beans, mangetout, salt and 50ml of water.

3 Cover and cook for a couple of minutes. Remove the lid and continue cooking for another minute or 2, uncovered, to allow any remaining water to evaporate. I prefer my vegetables with a little bite, but if you prefer them softer, you can cook them a little bit longer.

4 Toss together the vegetables and sprinkle with some sesame seeds.

African-inspired Feast

Kuku Paka

Ugali

Garlic Mogo Chips

Corn on the Cob

Kachumbari
(see page 193)

This feast is going to transport you to Kenya. As a child, I lived in both Tanzania and Kenya and I spent many a school holiday returning to visit family after we left. In fact, my husband and I even got married on a beautiful beach in Mombasa many moons ago! So it felt fitting that an African feast would have to be part of the recipe collection in this book. A lot of these dishes have an Indian influence, and I serve this feast with Kachumber see page 193 (or *kachumbari*, as it's called in Kenya). This particular recipe, along with a lot of the spices, was brought to East Africa through Indian workers who came to work there during the colonial era. So make these recipes and sit back, close your eyes and imagine yourself on the beautiful beaches of Mombasa.

'...make these recipes and sit back, close your eyes and imagine yourself on the beautiful beaches of Mombasa'

Kuku Paka

This is an East African/Indian fusion dish of charcoal-grilled chicken (usually cooked in a *jiko* – a Kenyan barbecue) in a spiced coconut curry sauce, and it is absolutely delicious! I've tried to simplify it by using a grill to char the chicken, but if you have a barbecue and can get it over coal it will totally elevate this dish.

SERVES 4–5

500g boneless, skinless chicken thighs, cut into cubes

1 tbsp rapeseed oil

1 red onion, chopped

2 large tomatoes, chopped

1 x 400ml tin of coconut milk

Juice of ½ lemon

25g fresh coriander, chopped, to serve

MARINADE

4cm piece of fresh ginger, chopped

8 cloves garlic, peeled

1 tsp turmeric

1 tsp ground cumin

1 tsp Kashmiri chilli powder

1 tsp ground coriander

1 tsp salt

2 tbsp rapeseed oil

1 chilli (optional)

1 First, add all the marinade ingredients to a blender with a tablespoon of water and blend until smooth. Set this paste aside.

2 Add the chicken to a large bowl. Add half of the marinade mixture and rub it into the chicken. Let it marinate in the fridge for an hour.

3 When you're ready to cook, spread the chicken out on a baking tray and grill it under a hot grill until you see black spots appear and the chicken is slightly charred. Set it aside.

4 Heat the oil in a pan over medium heat and add the onion. Cook it until it starts to brown, then add the rest of the marinade paste and cook for a minute before adding the chopped tomatoes. Once the tomatoes have softened, add the chicken and coconut milk to the pan and bring it to a simmer.

5 Finally, add a squeeze of lemon juice and a sprinkle of freshly chopped coriander to serve.

Make it vegan

Skip steps 2 and 3 and add 2 x 400g cans chickpeas instead of chicken in step 4.

Ugali

Ugali is a staple dish in East Africa and is enjoyed as an accompaniment to stews and curries instead of rice. It's made with cornmeal, which is produced by grinding dried sweetcorn to a powder – similar to polenta but ground more finely. The traditional way to eat it is with your hands. You scoop up a small ball of ugali and use your thumb to make a deep indent. Then you scoop up the curry into the indent you have created, and it goes straight into your mouth.

SERVES 4

140g water

200g fine cornmeal

1 Add the water to a large heavy-based saucepan and bring up to the boil. Once the water is boiling, reduce the heat to low. Gradually add the cornmeal, a couple of tablespoons at a time, to the simmering water while continuously stirring with a wooden spoon or a stiff whisk. Keep stirring vigorously to prevent lumps from forming. Ugali should be smooth and lump-free.

2 Continue to cook and stir the mixture on low heat for about 10 minutes. The ugali will start to thicken and pull away from the sides of the pan. To check if it's ready, wet your fingers and touch the surface of the ugali. If it's not sticky and doesn't stick to your fingers, it's done.

3 Remove the saucepan from the heat. Place a plate on top of the saucepan and flip it over to turn out the hot ugali onto the plate. Roughly shape it into a dome using your hands, this is the way it is served traditionally. Serve it right away.

Garlic Mogo Chips

Mogo, also known as cassava or yuca, is a starchy root vegetable widely consumed in Africa. If you ever visit Mombasa, mogo crisps are a famous street-food snack you have to try, which have been famously made fresh in a certain area for many years. These (very) garlicky mogo chips are one of my favourite ways to enjoy mogo. I tend to buy frozen mogo that has been already peeled and prepped, for ease, but you could use fresh too. The cooking time will be about 10 minutes less.

SERVES 4

400g frozen mogo

50g fresh coriander

8 cloves garlic, peeled

2 tbsp lemon juice

½ tsp salt

60ml rapeseed oil

1 Preheat the oven to 200°C, 180°C fan, gas mark 6.

2 Place the frozen mogo in a large pan of boiling water over medium-high heat. Cook for 25–30 minutes until it's soft but retains its shape. Be careful not to overcook it.

3 Drain the mogo and, once it has cooled slightly, cut it into large 'chips' or wedges. Arrange them in a spacious baking tray, ensuring they are lying flat in one layer – this is key to getting them crispy.

4 In a blender, combine the coriander, garlic, lemon juice, salt and oil. Blend until it forms a smooth sauce.

5 Drizzle half of the sauce over the mogo chips and toss to coat them thoroughly. Save the remaining paste for later. Bake in the oven for approximately 30 minutes or until the chips turn golden and crispy. Alternatively, air-fry at 180°C for 20 minutes.

6 Serve the mogo chips with a drizzle of the reserved garlic sauce.

Corn on the Cob

This is corn on the cob in all its beauty, as it is served on the beaches of Mombasa, with a wedge of lemon that you dip into the salt and chilli mix and then rub all over the corn. One of life's simple pleasures. Then enjoy the sweet, juicy kernels and think of the most beautiful beach with white sand!

P.S. I grew the corn in this photo – my first time growing it in the garden!

SERVES 4

4 corn on the cob

2 tsp chilli powder

½ tsp salt

1 lemon, cut into wedges

1 Remove the silks and outer husks from the corn – you might need to open the inner husks to do this – then wrap them back around the corn cob.

2 Boil the corn in a large pan of boiling water for about 10 minutes. Alternatively, cook each cob, in its husk, in the microwave for 4 minutes.

3 Ideally, you would cook the corn over coal on a barbecue or a Kenyan jiko, but my cheat way is to peel back the husks fully and pop them under a very hot grill or directly on the flame of the hob to give them a little char.

4 Mix the chilli powder and salt in a bowl. Serve the lemon wedges alongside the cooked corn and chilli/salt mix, ready to dip the wedges into the chilli salt and rub it all over each corn cob.

Italian-inspired Feast

Mushroom &
Asparagus
Risotto with
Burrata

Baked Courgette
Fries

Garlic Dough
Balls

Rocket &
Parmesan Salad

Tomato Salad

The final feast in this chapter is going to transport you to Italy! It is one of my favourite food travel destinations. I just love the beautiful fresh produce, the simplicity of the recipes, which allow the fresh flavours to shine through, and the olive oil … Nothing beats it!

I'm sharing some of my favourite food memories of Italy in these recipes. You can make some of them as stand-alone meals or make them all together for an Italian-inspired feast!

'This feast is going to transport you to Italy! '

Mushroom & Asparagus Risotto with Burrata

This delicious risotto is packed with veggies (mushrooms and asparagus) and served with the crispy courgettes and side salads, it's a delicious plant-packed meal full of colours and flavours. I sometimes serve the risotto with a fillet of pan-fried sea bass to make it even more special. I like to stir in a tablespoon of miso paste for extra umami, but you can skip this if you don't have it.

SERVES 6 AS PART OF THE 'FEAST' OR 4 IF MADE ALONE

1 tbsp olive oil

1 red onion, finely chopped

4 cloves garlic, finely chopped

250g chestnut mushrooms, sliced

150g shiitake mushrooms, sliced

250g arborio risotto rice

1 mushroom stock cube dissolved in 1l boiling water

300g asparagus, roughly chopped

100g parmesan, grated

1 tbsp miso paste (optional)

1 tsp black pepper

150g burrata

15g chopped chives, to serve

1 Heat the oil in a large pan over medium heat. Add the onions and sauté until soft and translucent. Add the garlic and sauté for a minute before adding all the mushrooms. Mix well. Once the mushrooms have softened, add the rice. Stir continuously for a couple of minutes until the rice is thoroughly coated in oil and develops a nutty flavour.

2 Next, add a quarter of the stock mixture to the rice. Stir over medium heat until all the liquid is absorbed by the rice, about 3–4 minutes. Add another quarter of the stock and repeat this process twice more. Add the final quarter of the stock along with the asparagus.

3 Once most of the final addition of liquid has been absorbed, stir in the parmesan, miso paste (if using) and black pepper.

4 Serve immediately with the burrata on top and a sprinkle of chives.

Baked Courgette Fries

Courgette fries that are baked but still as crispy as if they were fried! I know it's hard to believe, but follow these simple steps and you will have the crunchiest, crispiest courgette fries coated in my spiced parmesan coating. A great way to enjoy one of your five a day!

SERVES 6

50g panko breadcrumbs

30g parmesan/vegetarian parmesan, grated

1 tsp mixed dried herbs

½ tsp salt

½ tsp Kashmiri chilli powder

2 eggs

50g plain flour

500g courgettes

1 Preheat the oven to 220°C, 200°C fan, gas mark 7.

2 On a plate, mix the panko, parmesan, herbs, salt and chilli powder, spreading the mixture out flat. Crack the eggs into a bowl and whisk them. Place the flour on another plate.

3 Prepare the courgettes: halve them, then halve each half lengthwise again. Cut each quarter into 3 or 4, creating equal-sized wedges.

4 Dip each wedge first into the flour to coat, then into the egg, and finally into the panko mix. Press the panko mix onto each wedge to ensure full coating.

5 Place each coated wedge on an ovenproof wire rack. Bake in the oven for 10–15 minutes until crispy. The time may vary depending on the thickness of your wedges, so check every few minutes after 10 minutes.

6 Enjoy right away.

Garlic Dough Balls

These little garlic dough balls are so good. Make them in the air fryer in just 8 minutes! You can prep them ahead of time and leave them to prove. When you're ready, pop them into the oven and fill your kitchen with the beautiful aroma of freshly baked bread. I often use extra-virgin olive oil instead of butter to make my 'garlic butter'; it tastes incredible and is a great vegan alternative.

MAKES 14–16 BALLS

200g plain flour

3g fast-action yeast

1 tsp sugar

Pinch of salt

80–100ml warm water

GARLIC BUTTER/OIL

50g salted butter (room temp) or 50ml extra-virgin olive oil

3 cloves garlic, finely chopped

10g fresh chives, chopped

1 First, make the garlic butter/oil. Add all the ingredients to a bowl and mix well to incorporate. Set aside.

2 To make the dough, add the flour, yeast, sugar and salt to a bowl. Add 80ml of the warm water and work the ingredients together with your hands to make a quick dough. Knead well for 10 minutes (or use a stand mixer with a dough hook). Add a little more water if needed.

3 Take a small amount of the dough at a time, about the size of a large cherry tomato, and roll it into a ball with your hands. Place it on a lined baking tray, pop it into a cold oven and leave it to prove for 1–2 hours. They should roughly double in size by that time.

4 Preheat the oven to 200°C, 180°C fan, gas mark 6 and bake the dough balls for 8–10 minutes until golden. Alternatively, bake in the air fryer at 180°C for 8–10 minutes.

5 Serve with the garlic butter to dip, or brush the top of the rolls with the garlicky oil.

Rocket & Parmesan Salad

This is a super simple salad with maximum taste. The peppery rocket pairs so well with the balsamic vinegar and the creamy, salty parmesan shavings finish it off. It's a delicious fresh, light salad to go with the mushroom risotto whilst maximising on your plant points and five a day.

SERVES 6

2 tbsp extra-virgin olive oil

2 tbsp balsamic vinegar

½ tsp black pepper

150g rocket leaves

20g parmesan/vegetarian parmesan

1 Make the salad dressing by mixing the extra-virgin olive oil, balsamic vinegar and pepper in a small jar. Shake well.

2 When ready to serve, add the rocket to a large bowl.

3 Use a vegetable peeler to peel parmesan shavings onto the salad.

4 Drizzle over the dressing and serve right away.

Tomato Salad

I love tomato season, and when you have beautiful, plump, seasonal tomatoes you want their flavour to shine through. So I like to serve them just like this – with a generous drizzle of extra-virgin olive oil and a sprinkle of salt. Simplicity at its best.

SERVES 6

2 large beef tomatoes, thinly sliced

Pinch of sea-salt flakes

2 tbsp extra-virgin olive oil

a handful of fresh basil leaves, to serve

1 Arrange the tomato slices on a large plate, ensuring they are not overlapping too much.

2 Sprinkle a pinch of sea salt over the tomatoes and drizzle with olive oil.

3 Serve and enjoy!

Conversion charts

WEIGHT

Metric	Imperial
25g	1oz
50g	2oz
75g	3oz
100g	4oz
150g	5oz
175g	6oz
200g	7oz
225g	8oz
250g	9oz
300g	10oz
350g	12oz
400g	14oz
450g	1lb

LIQUIDS

Metric	Imperial	US cup
5ml	1 tsp	1 tsp
15ml	1 tbsp	1 tbsp
50ml	2fl oz	3 tbsp
60ml	2½fl oz	¼ cup
75ml	3fl oz	⅓ cup
100ml	4fl oz	scant ½ cup
125ml	4½fl oz	½ cup
150ml	5fl oz	⅔ cup
200ml	7fl oz	scant 1 cup
250ml	9fl oz	1 cup
300ml	½ pint	1¼ cups
350ml	12fl oz	1⅓ cups
400ml	¾ pint	1¾ cups
500ml	17fl oz	2 cups
600ml	1 pt	2½ cups

MEASUREMENTS

Metric	Imperial
5cm	2in
10cm	4in
13cm	5in
15cm	6in
18cm	7in
20cm	8in
25cm	10in
30cm	12in

Acknowledgements

To my Mum and Papa, who initiated and fed my curiosity around food from an early age and whose story always reminds me that absolutely anything is possible and that glass ceilings are made to be broken.

For Sammy, my rock, my best friend and my biggest cheerleader. Thank you for supporting me and encouraging me to follow my dream. Your constant encouragement and guidance when I felt like giving up were invaluable.

Kush and Yash, my constant inspiration, always teaching me to better myself and guiding me in a way that only the innocence of children can and for also being so brutally honest with recipe feedback!

To Cassie Best and all at BBC *Good Food*, my heartfelt gratitude for showcasing my recipes on the UK's biggest food platform, and helping me to spread my message to a broader audience.

To my editor, Duncan Proudfoot, thank you for putting up with ALL the edits and changes so graciously! For turning my vision of a cookbook into reality and for all the helpful advice and expert tips. To Andrew Barron for transforming my manuscript into my dream, illustrated cookbook. To the team at Palazzo, especially Kaz Harrison and Mel Sambells for championing me always.

Thank you to Jon Stefani for being my guru with navigating the world of publishing since day one. I couldn't have done this without your encouragement.

To Elaine Macaninch for lending her years of nutritional expertise to the nutrition chapter.

To Raakesh Katwa for the beautiful photos and memories of my family and me.

Finally, thank YOU for purchasing my book and welcoming my recipes into your homes. Without the support of the wonderful community that is *Dr Chintal's Kitchen* I wouldn't be here. To hold a hardback copy of my own cookbook was something I could never have imagined in my wildest dreams five years ago. It's thanks to each and every one of you that my long-standing dream has become a reality.

I will forever be grateful. Thank you!

Chintal x

References

1 National Dental Epidemiology Programme (NDEP) for England: oral health survey of 5-year-old children 2022 [Internet]. GOV.UK.

2 NHS Digital. National Child Measurement Programme, England, 2021/22 school year [Internet]. NHS Digital. 2022.

3 Perng W, Conway R, Mayer-Davis E, Dabelea D. Youth-Onset Type 2 Diabetes: The epidemiology of an awakening epidemic. Diabetes Care. 2023 Mar 1;46(3):490-9.

4 AfN Inter-Professional Working Group On Medical Nutrition Education Association for Nutrition UK Undergraduate Curriculum In Nutrition for Medical Doctors [Internet]. 2021. Available from: https://www.associationfornutrition. org/wp-content/uploads/2021/10/2021-UK-Undergraduate-Curriculum-in-Nutrition-for-Medical-Doctors-FINAL.pdf

5 Tan J, Atamanchuk L, Rao T, Sato K, Crowley J, Ball L. Exploring culinary medicine as a promising method of nutritional education in medical school: a scoping review. BMC Medical Education. 2022 Dec;22(1):1–24.

6 Diabetes UK. Low-carb diets for people with diabetes (2021) [Internet]. Diabetes UK. 2021. Available from: https://www. diabetes.org.uk/professionals/position-statements-reports/food-nutrition-lifestyle/low-carb-diets-for-people-with-diabetes

7 Katz DL. Best Diet For Health? Careful, It Bites! [Internet]. Forbes. [cited 2023 Sep 28]. Available from: https://www.forbes. com/sites/davidkatz/2016/10/05/ best-diet-for-health-careful-it-bites/

8 Tieri M, Ghelfi F, Vitale M, Vetrani C, Marventano S, Lafranconi A, Godos J, Titta L, Gambera A, Alonzo E, Sciacca S. Whole grain consumption and human health: an umbrella review of observational studies. International *Journal of Food Sciences and Nutrition.* 2020 Aug 17;71(6):668–77.

9 Khan J, Khan MZ, Ma Y, Meng Y, Mushtaq A, Shen Q, Xue Y. Overview of the composition of whole grains' phenolic acids and dietary fibre and their effect on chronic non-communicable diseases. *International Journal of Environmental Research and Public Health.* 2022 Mar 5;19(5):3042.

10 Begum S, Miraj S, Jan A, Shah S, Ali F, Zeb F. Polycystic Ovarian Syndrome (PCOS) and Low Glycemic Diet-An Updated Review of literature. *Journal of Food and Dietetics Research.* 2023 Mar 10;3(1):1–4.

11 Chiavaroli L, Lee D, Ahmed A, Cheung A, Khan TA, Blanco S, Mirrahimi A, Jenkins DJ, Livesey G, Wolever TM, Rahelić D. Effect of low glycaemic index or load dietary patterns on glycaemic control and cardiometabolic risk factors in diabetes: systematic review and meta-analysis of randomised controlled trials. *BMJ.* 2021 Aug 5;374.

12 Lennerz B, Lennerz JK. Food addiction, high-glycemic-index carbohydrates, and obesity. Clinical chemistry. 2018 Jan 1;64(1):64–71.

13 Public Health England. Government Dietary Recommendations Government Recommendations for Energy and Nutrients for Males and Females Aged 1–18 Years and 19+ Years [Internet]. GOV. UK. Public Health England; 2016 Aug. Available from: https://assets.publishing. service.gov.uk/government/uploads/ system/uploads/attachment_data/ file/618167/government_dietary_ recommendations.pdf

14 Sievenpiper, J.L.; Kendall, C.W.C.; Esfahani, A.; Wong, J.M.W.; Carleton, A.J.; Jiang, H.Y.; Bazinet, R.P.; Vidgen, E.; Jenkins, D.J.A. Effect of non-oil-seed pulses on glycaemic control: A systematic review and meta-analysis of randomised controlled experimental trials in people with and without diabetes. *Diabetologia* 2009, 52, 1479–1495.

15 Gunness P, Gidley MJ. Mechanisms underlying the cholesterol-lowering properties of soluble dietary fibre polysaccharides. Food & function. 2010;1(2):149–55.

16 Fogelholm M, Anderssen S, Gunnarsdottir I, Lahti-Koski M. Dietary macronutrients and food consumption as determinants of long-term weight change in adult populations: a systematic literature review. Food & nutrition research. 2012 Jan 1;56(1):19103.

17 Bradbury KE, Appleby PN, Key TJ. Fruit, vegetable, and fiber intake in relation to cancer risk: findings from the European Prospective Investigation into Cancer and Nutrition (EPIC). *The American Journal of Clinical Nutrition.* 2014 Jul 1;100(suppl_1):394S-8S.

18 Hartley L, May MD, Loveman E, Colquitt JL, Rees K. Dietary fibre for the primary prevention of cardiovascular disease. Cochrane Database of Systematic Reviews. 2016(1).

19 Yao B, Fang H, Xu W, Yan Y, Xu H, Liu Y, Mo M, Zhang H, Zhao Y. Dietary fiber intake and risk of type 2 diabetes: a dose–response analysis of prospective studies. *European Journal of Epidemiology.* 2014 Feb;29:79–88.

20 Public Health England. NDNS: results from years 9 to 11 (2016 to 2017 and 2018 to 2019) [Internet]. GOV.UK. 2020. Available from: https://www.gov.uk/government/ statistics/ndns-results-from-years-9-to-11-2016-to-2017-and-2018-to-2019

21 Hooper L, Martin N, Jimoh OF, Kirk C, Foster E, Abdelhamid AS. Reduction in saturated fat intake for cardiovascular disease. Cochrane database of systematic reviews. 2020(8).

22 Giosuè A, Calabrese I, Vitale M, Riccardi G, Vaccaro O. Consumption of dairy foods and cardiovascular disease: A systematic review. Nutrients. 2022 Feb 16;14(4):831.

23 Martínez-González MA, Salas-Salvadó J, Estruch R, Corella D, Fitó M, Ros E, Predimed Investigators. Benefits of the Mediterranean diet: insights from the PREDIMED study. Progress in cardiovascular diseases. 2015 Jul 1;58(1):50–60.

24 Public Health England. The Eatwell Guide [Internet]. gov.uk. Public Health England; 2016. Available from: https://www. gov.uk/government/publications/ the-eatwell-guide

25 Omega-3 and omega-6 fats [Internet]. The Vegan Society. 2019. Available from: https://www.vegansociety.com/resources/ nutrition-and-health/nutrients/ omega-3-and-omega-6-fats

26 Mori TA. Marine OMEGA-3 fatty acids in the prevention of cardiovascular disease. Fitoterapia. 2017 Nov 1;123:51–8.

27 Jimenez-Lopez C, Carpena M, Lourenço-Lopes C, Gallardo-Gomez M, Lorenzo JM, Barba FJ, Prieto MA, Simal-Gandara J. Bioactive compounds and quality of extra virgin olive oil. Foods. 2020 Jul 28;9(8):1014.

28 British Nutrition Foundation. Nutrition Requirements Lower Reference Nutrient Intakes (LRNIs) [Internet]. 2021. Available from: https://www.nutrition.org.uk/media/1z2ekndj/nutrition-requirements-update.pdf

29 Baum JI, Kim IY, Wolfe RR. Protein consumption and the elderly: what is the optimal level of intake?. Nutrients. 2016 Jun 8;8(6):359.

30 Managing Malnutrition: Protein Foods [Internet]. www.malnutritionpathway.co.uk. Available from: https://www.malnutritionpathway.co.uk/proteinfoods

31 British Nutrition Foundation. Children – British Nutrition Foundation [Internet]. www.nutrition.org.uk. 2022. Available from: https://www.nutrition.org.uk/life-stages/children/

32 Willett W, Rockström J, Loken B, Springmann M, Lang T, Vermeulen S, Garnett T, Tilman D, DeClerck F, Wood A, Jonell M. Food in the Anthropocene: the EAT–Lancet Commission on healthy diets from sustainable food systems. *The Lancet.* 2019 Feb 2;393(10170):447–92.

33 Blumfield M, Mayr H, De Vlieger N, Abbott K, Starck C, Fayet-Moore F, Marshall S. Should We 'Eat a Rainbow'? An Umbrella Review of the Health Effects of Colorful Bioactive Pigments in Fruits and Vegetables. Molecules. 2022 Jun 24;27(13):4061.

34 Alissa EM, Ferns GA. Dietary fruits and vegetables and cardiovascular diseases risk. Critical reviews in food science and nutrition. 2017 Jun 13;57(9):1950–62.

35 Li M, Fan Y, Zhang X, Hou W, Tang Z. Fruit and vegetable intake and risk of type 2 diabetes mellitus: meta-analysis of prospective cohort studies. *BMJ open.* 2014 Nov 1;4(11):e005497.

36 McDonald D, Hyde E, Debelius JW, Morton JT, Gonzalez A, Ackermann G, Aksenov AA, Behsaz B, Brennan C, Chen Y, DeRight Goldasich L. American gut: an open platform for citizen science microbiome research. Msystems. 2018 Jun 3(3):10–128.

37 Siervo M, Lara J, Chowdhury S, Ashor A, Oggioni C, Mathers JC. Effects of the Dietary Approach to Stop Hypertension (DASH) diet on cardiovascular risk factors: a systematic review and meta-analysis. British Journal of Nutrition. 2015 113(1):1–5.

38 NICE. Vitamin D prevention and management of deficiency [Internet]. NICE. Available from: https://cks.nice.org.uk/topics/vitamin-d-deficiency-in-adults/management/prevention/

39 Webb AR, Kazantzidis A, Kift RC, Farrar MD, Wilkinson J, Rhodes LE. Colour counts: sunlight and skin type as drivers of vitamin D deficiency at UK latitudes. Nutrients. 2018 Apr 7;10(4):457.

40 NHS. Healthy Start [Internet]. Healthystart.nhs.uk. NHS; 2019. Available from: https://www.healthystart.nhs.uk/

41 NHS. Vitamins for children [Internet]. nhs.uk. 2020. Available from: https://www.nhs.uk/conditions/baby/weaning-and-feeding/vitamins-for-children/

42 Lin LY, Smeeth L, Langan S, Warren-Gash C. Distribution of vitamin D status in the UK: a cross-sectional analysis of UK Biobank. BMJ open. 2021 Jan 1;11(1):e038503.

43 Key priorities | Maternal and child nutrition | Guidance | NICE [Internet]. www.nice.org.uk. Available from: https://www.nice.org.uk/guidance/ph11/chapter/1-key-priorities#:~:text=Advise%20them%20to%20take%20400

44 de Vos WM, Tilg H, Van Hul M, Cani PD. Gut microbiome and health: mechanistic insights. Gut. 2022 May 1;71(5):1020–32.

45 Gilbert JA, Blaser MJ, Caporaso JG, Jansson JK, Lynch SV, Knight R. Current understanding of the human microbiome. Nature medicine. 2018 Apr 1;24(4):392–400

46 Dimidi E, Cox SR, Rossi M, Whelan K. Fermented foods: definitions and characteristics, impact on the gut microbiota and effects on gastrointestinal health and disease. Nutrients. 2019 Aug 5;11(8):1806.

47 Nagarajan M, Rajasekaran B, Venkatachalam K. Microbial metabolites in fermented food products and their potential benefits. *International Food Research Journal.* 2022 May 1;29(3):466–86.

48 BDA. Probiotics [Internet]. www.bda.uk.com. Available from: https://www.bda.uk.com/resource/probiotics.html

49 Kaiser J, van Daalen KR, Thayyil A, Cocco MT, Caputo D, Oliver-Williams C. A systematic review of the association between vegan diets and risk of cardiovascular disease. *The Journal of Nutrition.* 2021 Jun;151(6):1539–52.

50 Morais S, Costa A, Albuquerque G, Araújo N, Pelucchi C, Rabkin CS, Liao LM, Sinha R, Zhang ZF, Hu J, Johnson KC. Salt intake and gastric cancer: a pooled analysis within the Stomach cancer Pooling (StoP) Project. Cancer Causes & Control. 2022 May;33(5):779–91.

51 Caudarella R, Vescini F, Rizzoli E, Francucci CM. Salt intake, hypertension, and osteoporosis. *Journal of Endocrinological Investigation.* 2009 Jan 1;32(4 Suppl):15–20.

52 Lane MM, Davis JA, Beattie S, Gómez-Donoso C, Loughman A, O'Neil A, Jacka F, Berk M, Page R, Marx W, Rocks T. Ultra-processed food and chronic noncommunicable diseases: a systematic review and meta-analysis of 43 observational studies. Obesity Reviews. 2021 Mar;22(3):e13146.

53 Taneri PE, Wehrli F, Roa-Díaz ZM, Itodo OA, Salvador D, Raeisi-Dehkordi H, Bally L, Minder B, Kiefte-de Jong JC, Laine JE, Bano A. Association between ultra-processed food intake and all-cause mortality: a systematic review and meta-analysis. *American Journal of Epidemiology.* 2022 Jul;191(7):1323–35.

54 Mertens E, Colizzi C, Peñalvo JL. Ultra-processed food consumption in adults across Europe. *European Journal of Nutrition.* 2022 Apr;61(3):1521–39.

55 Monteiro C, Cannon G, Levy R, Moubarac JC, Jaime P, Martins A, et al. The Food System Food classification. Public health NOVA. The star shines bright. World Nutrition [Internet]. 2016;7(1–3). Available from: https://archive.wphna.org/wp-content/uploads/2016/01/WN-2016-7-1-3-28-38-Monteiro-Cannon-Levy-et-al-NOVA.pdf

56 Farmer N, Touchton-Leonard K, Ross A. Psychosocial benefits of cooking interventions: a systematic review. Health Education & Behavior. 2018 Apr;45(2):167–80.

Index